GREAT

—

RUSSIAN

———

MUSICIANS

—

GREAT

—

RUSSIAN

—

MUSICIANS

—

FROM RUBINSTEIN TO RICHTER

Ernst Zaltsberg

mosaic press

National Library of Canada Cataloguing in Publication Data

Zaltsberg, Ernst 1937-
    Great Russian Musicians: from Rubinstein to Richter

Includes index.
ISBN 0-88962-756-8

    I. Title.

OS3523.A4415 2002   811'.6   C 2002-901114-0

Published by Mosaic Press, offices and warehouse at 1252 Speers Road, Units 1 and 2, Oakville, Ontario, L6L 5N9, Canada and Mosaic Press, PMB 145, 4500 Witmer Industrial Estates, Niagara Falls, NY, 14305-1386, U.S.A.

Mosaic Press acknowledges the assistance of the Canada Council and the Department of Canadian Heritage, Government of Canada for their support of our publishing programme.

Copyright © 2002 Ernst Zaltzberg
Printed and Bound in Canada.
ISBN 0-88962-792-4

Mosaic Press in Canada:
1252 Speers Road, Units 1 & 2,
Oakville, Ontario
L6L 5N9
Phone/Fax: 905-825-2130
mosaicpress@on.aibn.com

Mosaic Press in U.S.A.:
4500 Witmer Industrial Estates
PMB 145, Niagara Falls, NY
14305-1386
Phone/Fax: 1-800-387-8992
mosaicpress@on.aibn.com

Le Conseil des Arts | The Canada Council
du Canada | for the Arts

www.mosaic-press.com

To my Mother and Madeline

Ernst Zaltsberg

CONTENTS

INTRODUCTION

This book is not a history of Russian performing arts but rather a set of biographical and artistic sketches of a few remarkable musicians. The selection of musicians in this book is not based on some ranking or comparison with other great performers but rather reflects the author's personal taste and passion.

All the musicians in this volume were born in the Russian Empire before the Revolution of 1917. It is interesting to note that many of them - A. Rubinstein, A. Brodsky, R. Pasternak, H. Neuhaus, S. Samosud, N. Milstein, D. Oistrakh, E. Gilels and S. Richter - were born and raised in the southern provinces of the Empire.

With the exception of S. Richter, who was not inclined to teach, the other musicians discussed in this book showed were to be not only great performers but also outstanding teachers. A. Rubinstein was a founder of the first Russian Conservatory in St. Petersburg and a great educator and teacher. Among his pupils were P. Tchaikovsky, F. Blumenfeld, J. Hofmann, V. Timanoff and T. Carreño.

W. Landowska taught almost all the harpsichordists who performed on the concert stage from the 1930s till the 1950s. H. Neuhaus' students included S. Richter, E. Gilels, Y. Zak and the prize-winners of almost all international piano competitions. D. Oistrakh prepared such outstanding violinists as N. Beilina, E. Grach, O. Kagan, G. Kremer, O. Krisa, V. Pikaisen, and I. Oistrakh.

M. Yudina was not only a great performer, but also a remarkable teacher, loved and admired by her students.

Rubinstein was the greatest Russian Romantic and had a tremendous influence on several generations of Russian musicians. Thus, A. Rubinstein encouraged the young R. Pasternak (née Kaufman) to pursue her musical education and performing career and invited her to give concerts in St. Petersburg and Moscow. One of his former students, F. Teytelbaum-Levinson, was the first piano teacher of M. Yudina. While A. Rubinstein was the foremost Romantic, Heinrich and Stanislav Neuhaus were among the last representatives of this movement. Other musicians such as N. Milstein, D. Oistrakh and E. Gilels represented the post-Romantic movement, which was characterized by a balance between emotions, inspiration and intelligence, and a strong emphasis on structural clarity. Of special interest is the highly intellectual and philosophical performing style of M. Yudina and S. Richter, especially in his later years.

Each of the musicians chosen for this book had their preferred repertoire and favourite composers. For example, H. and S. Neuhaus were in their element playing F. Chopin and A. Scriabin, while J. Bach, L. Beethoven and modern composers featured largely in M. Yudina's repertoire. S. Richter was perfect in a wide range of piano music, especially in the French Impressionists and S. Prokofiev, while E. Gilels dedicated himself to mighty compositions by R. Schumann, J. Brahms, L. Beethoven and P. Tchaikovsky. W. Landowska had rediscovered Baroque music and propagated it vigorously during her performing career.

Except for A. Rubinstein, all of the musicians in this volume belonged to the twentieth-century and its tempestuous history. W. Landowska left the Russian Empire and settled in Paris in 1900, and in 1940 she left war- striken France and fled to the USA. R. Pasternak moved from Russia to Germany in 1921 and died, in 1939, in England. N. Milstein went on a concert tour abroad in 1925 and never returned to Russia. He became an American citizen in 1942.

Other musicians, including S. Samosud, H. and S. Neuhaus, M. Yudina, D. Oistrakh, S. Richter and E. Gilels, remained in the former USSR. While Gilels and Oistrakh became part of the Soviet musical establishment and demonstrated devotion and loyalty to the Soviet totalitarian régime, Yudina and Richter dissociated themselves from the system and opposed its doctrines.

I had the privilege of hearing live performances by the majority of the musicians in this book. I followed the performing careers of D. Oistrakh, S. Richter and E. Gilels for decades, and they became an important part of my life and for my generation. Although I rarely heard S. Samosud, H. Neuhaus, S. Neuhaus, M. Yudina and N. Milstein, each of them made a significant contribution to my understanding of music and creativity.

1

1

R<small>UBINSTEIN WAS BORN ON</small> November 28th, 1829, in the village of Vikhvatinyetz in Moldavia, which at that time was a Russian province. His father Gregory was born in Berdichev, Ukraine, and his mother Kaleria (née Levenstein) was from Prussian Silesia. Both parents were fluent in Russian, Yiddish and German.

Anton Rubinstein

When Anton was one and a half years old, the entire family, according to the wish of his grandfather Roman, was baptized. In 1834 Gregory moved to Moscow with the family, where he established a small pencil manufacturing business. Next year, Kaleria gave birth to Nicolai, who, like Anton, possessed a great musical talent. Kaleria herself was an advanced amateur pianist, and when Anton turned five, she started to teach him piano. After one year of studying with Kaleria, the boy was accepted in the class of the outstanding Moscow teacher Aleksander Villoing. Later Anton remembered: "He was my single teacher, I did not have any others... During all my life I had not met a better one."[1]

Rubinstein's first public performance took place on July 11, 1839, in the Petrovsky park in Moscow. The program included compositions by J. Hummel, S. Thalberg, F. Liszt, J. Field and A. Henselt.

At the end of that year, accompanied by Villoing, Anton went to Paris to enter the famous Paris Conservatory. However, the Conservatory's Director, Cherubini refused to audition him because he was too young. Anton continued to study with Villoing and played in Parisian music salons and in wealthy patrons' houses. At the end of 1840, he performed at the Salle Erard for an audience that included Liszt, Chopin and Meyerbeer. Liszt wrote about this event: "Rubinstein is a brilliant phenomenon in the field of piano virtuosity, and he will be my successor."[2] The day after the concert, Chopin invited Anton to his studio where he played his compositions for the boy.

After the Paris début, Anton, accompanied by his teacher, went on a long concert tour through Western Europe, which included performances in Vienna, Budapest, Berlin, London, Warsaw, Stockholm and Christiania (Oslo). He returned to Moscow in 1843.

Shortly before Anton's return to Moscow, Liszt had given a few concerts in the Russian capital. Kaleria approached him and asked his advice about her sons' future. Liszt suggested that they should continue their musical education in Germany. In order to raise the necessary money for such a journey, Anton made a concert tour through Russia. In St. Petersburg both Anton and Nicolai played for Tsar Nicolai I and his family at the Winter Palace.

In the spring of 1844, the brothers and Kaleria went to Berlin, where they received a hearty welcome from Meyerbeer and Mendelssohn. They studied with the famous teacher and theorist Siegfriend Dehn, who, several years earlier, had given harmony lessons to the greatRussian composer Mikhail Glinka. Meyerbeer wrote of the Rubinsteins' study with Dehn: "These youths studied with such zeal that their achievements in harmony and counterpoint could be termed amazing... Considering their natural gift, I could predict a brilliant musical career for them in the future; they would be a great credit to their Motherland Russia."[3]

The brothers' general education in Berlin was limited to lessons on the catechism and Russian grammar with the priest from the local Greek Orthodox church. However, due to his keen mind, perfect memory and extensive self-education, Anton soon became a sophisticated man, fluent in several European languages and well acquainted with European literature, art and philosophy.

In the summer of 1846, Kaleria got a message from Moscow about her husband's serious illness. She and Nicolai rushed to Russia, but upon arrival in the capital they found Gregory dead. He left a significant debt, and in order to pay it, Kaleria took a position as a governess in a private school, while Nicolai went on a concert tour.

Meanwhile Anton remained in Berlin and continued his study with Dehn and later with another famous theory professor, Adolph Marx. Out of money, the young musician went to Vienna where he desperately tried to make a living. He taught piano, composed music for commissions, wrote literary reviews, critical and philosophical essays. However, his financial situation remained difficult. When the 1848 Revolution erupted in Europe, Rubinstein returned to St. Petersburg. Here he gave private piano lessons, recitals and often played for the Tsar's family. In this circle Anton found a wealthy and influential patroness, the Grand Duchess Yelena Pavlovna, a sister-in-law of Tsar Nicolai. In 1852, she offered Rubinstein the position of court pianist. His duties were not very time consuming, so he had a plenty of time to practise piano and compose. By that time, Anton had written several operas, piano concertos and sonatas and numerous piano miniatures.

By the early 1850s, Anton Rubinstein had become a leading figure in the musical life of St. Petersburg. He gave recitals, played as an accompanist with many famous singers and instrumentalists touring the northern capital, and conducted the local symphony orchestra. He often spent his summer holidays in the Grand Duchess' Palace on the Kammennyi Ostrov (Stone Island) in St. Petersburg, where she provided him with a very stimulating and comfortable environment.

In 1854, Rubinstein went to Western Europe to promote his compositions. His first stop was in Weimar, where he stayed in Liszt's house. The two celebrated pianists gave several public performances together. Liszt also conducted the German premiere of Rubinstein's opera *Die Sibirischen Jäger* (*The Siberian Hunters*) at the Weimar Opera Theatre.

On December 14th, 1854, Rubinstein gave a recital at the famous Gewandhaus in Leipzig, which was the starting point for his triumphal European concert tour, during which he gave concerts in Germany, France, England and Austria-Hungary.

While performing at concerts in Vienna in May, 1856, Anton published the article entitled *Die Komponisten Russlands (Russian Com-*

posers) in the local journal *Blätter für Muzik, Theater und Kunst.* In this publication Rubinstein praised his Russian colleagues and especially Glinka, whom he called "a Russian Schubert". However, according to Rubinstein, even such a genius as Glinka had completely failed to create a Russian national opera. This article prompted a harsh response in Russian media and the Russian musical community. Thus, Glinka proclaimed: "An insolent Jew has discredited my little old lady, the opera *Zhizn' za Tsarya (A Life for the Tsar)*."[4]

Despite his heavy concert schedule, Anton continued composing. In 1854 he completed one of the best of his compositions, the vocal cycle *Persian Songs* to verses by Mizra-Shafi Vazekh. This piece is still heard on concert stages today. Two years later, Rubinstein's oratorio *Paradise Lost*, based on John Milton's poem, was premiered under Liszt's baton.

In the fall of 1856, the Grand Duchess Yelena Pavlovna asked Rubinstein to return to Russia to take part in the coronation of the new Tsar, Alexander II. When the celebrations were over, the Grand Duchess invited the musician to follow her to France and to stay at her villa in Nice. There, in the winter of 1856-1857, he was thinking of how to develop a comprehensive system of musical education in Russia. He discussed this subject extensively with the Grand Duchess. Having enlisted her aid, Rubinstein began putting his ideas into practice.

In 1858, Rubenstein established the Singing Academy. The next year, he founded the Russian Musical Society (RMS). In 1860, music classes under Rubinstein's directorship began at the RMS. Among the teachers of this new school were such distinguished musicians as Theodor Leschetizky (piano) and Henrik Wieniawski (violin). In 1862, these classes were transformed into the St. Petersburg Conservatory, the first educational institution of this sort in Russia. Rubinstein was appointed its director. Among the first Conservatory students were Tchaikovsky and Annette Essipova. In 1866 N. Rubenstein established the second Russian Conservatory in Moscow.

Rubinstein's duties at the St. Petersburg Conservatory were diverse and time-consuming. In addition to his directorship, he taught orchestration, piano, chamber music and conducted the Conservatory choir and orchestra. On principle, his teaching was free of charge. Moreover, he donated half his director's salary to a fund established to support students from low-income families.

Rubinstein took his director's duties very seriously, including various administrative and financial obligations. This work came to take up almost all his time and led to a significant reduction in his concert activity. However, he was still able to devote some of his time to composition. In 1863, his opera *Feramorse* was premiered in Dresden, and next year in St. Petersburg he gave the first performance of his Piano Concerto No. 4 (Op. 70).

In 1865, Anton married Vera Tchekuanova. Beautiful though Vera was, this marriage was not a happy one and the couple separated in 1891. None of their three children inherited any of their father's musical talents.

The establishment of the first Russian conservatories prompted various responses among the Russian musical community. Some of its members strongly supported Rubinstein's initiative, while a group of young nationalist composers - Balakirev, Borodin, Cui, Mussorgsky andRimsky-Korsakov, known as "the Five" - insisted that European-style musical education would prevent the true development of a national Russian music.

Owing to this criticism, which was blown out of proportion by the Russian media, and disagreements with many of the professors about the goal and the substance of musical education, Rubinstein resigned from the Conservatory in 1867 and resumed the concert activity. He performed extensively in both Russia and Western Europe, and particularly in Germany, where he was always given a warm reception. He now significantly extended his piano repertoire which included his own compositions but also the music of his predecessors and contemporaries.

In 1868, Anton gave several recitals in London, where he also played chamber music together with Leopold Auer (violin) and Alfredo Piatti (cello). Later, Auer wrote on their performance of Beethoven's *Archduke* Trio: "...To this day I can recall how Rubinstein sat down at the piano, his leonine head thrown slightly back, and began the five opening measures of the principal theme... It seemed to me I had never before heard the piano really played. The grandeur of style..., the beauty of tone his softness of touch secured, the art with which he manipulated the pedal, are indescribable..."[5]

As usual, Rubinstein successfully combined concert performance with composing. In the late 1860s he composed the tone poem *Ivan the Terrible*, the oratorio *The Tower of Babel* and numerous piano pieces, including Fantasy Op. 84.

At that time, some "thaw" in the relationship between Rubinstein and "the Five" became evident. The première of *Ivan the Terrible* was conducted by Balakirev, and Cui, who was usually a caustic critic of Rubinstein's compositions, gave this performance a favourable review. Meanwhile, Rubinstein performed the music of "the Five" in his piano and orchestral concerts quite often, regardless of their criticism of his own compositions.

However, this "thaw" was short-lived. On September 15th, 1871, the Rubinstein brothers performed Anton's new opera *The Demon* for "the Five". His colleagues' more than cool treatment of the opera deeply affected the composer. *The Demon* was also banned by the censorship committee and could not be produced in any of the Imperial theatres.

Deeply depressed by this development, Rubinstein accepted an offer from Vienna's *Gesellschaft der Musikfreunde* (Friends of the Music Society) and became its artistic director. In Vienna, his directorial duties included the Society's concert programming, conducting the choir and orchestra, and presenting his own piano recitals.

One of these recitals, which included a performance of his Variations, Op. 88, was heard by Liszt and Hans von Bülow. Liszt described the concert as "absolutely brilliant", while von Bülow wrote "...the furiously artistic Variations Op. 88 were played in a superLisztian manner that deeply impressed me."[6]

To achieve financial independence, Rubinstein resigned from his position in Vienna and signed a contract for 200 concerts in North America. In August 1872, he sailed from Liverpool to New York. This tour became a concert marathon: in eight months, the pianist gave 216 performances in 60 cities and towns across America. Besides big cities such as New York, Boston, Philadelphia, Chicago, Washington, Baltimore, and Detroit, he appeared in many small cities and towns, where, in many cases, he was the first pianist to play classical repertoire for the local audiences. At the end of this enormous tour, Rubinstein gave seven farewell "Historical concerts" in nine days in New York. The programs included piano literature from Bach to Liszt. The seventh and last concert was completely devoted to Rubinstein's own music. These concerts were a prototype of the cycle under the same title he would later perform in Europe.

Upon returning from the New World, Anton performed concerts tirelessly in both Russia and Western Europe. While on tour in Spain, he learned of his brother Nicolai's death in Paris on March 11, 1881, at the age of forty-five. This sad news deeply shook the elder Rubinstein. To commemorate his brother, Anton conducted three concerts with the RMS Symphony in Moscow which were to have been given by Nicolai. At the first concert, according to Nicolai's will, the orchestra and chorus performed Schumann's *Requiem*.

In the 1880s, the pianist enjoyed the peak of his fame. In 1885-1886 he realized one of the most ambitious projects in the history of piano playing. That year, he performed a cycle of "Historical concerts" covering keyboard répertoire from the eighteenth-century English virginalists to contemporary Russian composers such as Balakirev, Tchaikovsky and Rubinstein. The cycle was heard in St. Petersburg, Moscow, Vienna, Berlin, Leipzig, London and Paris.

It is interesting to note the programs of these unique series:

RECITAL I

Byrd	*The Carman's Whistle*
Bull	*The King's Hunting Jig*
Couperin	*La Ténébreuse, La Favorite, La Fleurie, Le Bavolet Flottant, La Bandoline, Le Reveil-matin*
Rameau	*Le Rappel des oiseaux, La Poule,* Gavotte et Variations
D. Scarlatti	Fugue in G minor (Cat's Fugue), Sonata in A major
J.S. Bach	Chromatic Fantasia and Fugue, B-flat Gigue from Partita No. 1, Sarabande and Gavotte in G minor from *English* Suite No. 3, Preludes and Fugues in C minor and D major, Preludes in E-flat minor, E-flat major, and B-flat minor from *The Well-Tempered Clavier*

Handel	Air et Variations (*The Harmonious Blacksmith*) from the Suite in E major, Fugue from the Suite in E minor, Sarabande and Passacaille from the Suite in G major, Gigue from the Suite in A major, Aria con variazioni in D minor
C.P.E. Bach	Rondo in B minor, *La Xénophone, Sibylle, Les* Langueurs Tendres, La Complaisante
Haydn	Variations in F minor
Mozart	Fantasy in C minor, K. 475, Gigue in G major, K. 574, Rondo in A minor, K. 511, Rondo *alla Turca* from the Sonata in A major, K. 331

RECITAL II

Beethoven	8 sonatas: Op. 27, No. 2, *Moonlight*, Op. 31, No. 2, *Tempest*, Op. 53, *Waldstein*, Op. 57, *Appasionata*, Op. 90, Op. 101, Op. 109, Op. 111

RECITAL III

Schubert	Fantasia in C major, *Wanderer, Six Moments musicaux*, Minuet in B minor from the G major Sonata, Impromptu in C minor, Impromptu in E flat major
Weber	Sonata No. 2 in A-flat major, *Momento capriccioso*, Invitation to the Dance, Polacca brillante
Mendelssohn	*Variations serieuses*, Op. 54, Caprice in E minor, Op. 16, No. 2, 11 *Songs without Words, Scherzo a capriccio* in F-sharp minor

RECITAL IV

Schumann	Fantasia in C major, Op. 17, *Kreisleriana*, Op. 16, *Symphonic Etudes*, Op. 13, Sonata in F-sharp minor, Op. 11, *Des Abends, In der Nacht, Traumeswirren, Warum?* from *Fantasiestücke*, Op.12, *The Prophet Bird*, Op. 82, No. 7, *Romanze* in D minor, Op. 32, No. 3, *Carnaval*, Op. 9

RECITAL V

Clementi	Sonata in B-flat major
Field	3 Nocturnes in E-flat major, A major, B-flat major
Moscheles	4 *Etudes caractéristiques*, Op. 95
Henselt	*Poème d'amour*, Op. 3, Berceuse, *Liebeslied*, Op. 5, No. 11, *La Fontaine*, Op. 6, No. 1, *Schmerz im Glück*, Op. 6, No. 2, *Were I a Bird*, Op. 2, No. 6
Liszt	Etude de concert, No. 3 in D-flat major, *Valsecaprice, Consolations* in D major and D-flat major, *Au bord d'une source*, Hungar ian Rhapso dies, Nos. 6 and 12, *Soirées muicales* (after Rossini), *La Gita* in gondola, La regata Veneziana, La serenata, La Danza
Schubert-Liszt	*Auf dem Wasser zu singen, Ständchen von Shakespeare, Soirée de Vienne* in A major
Meyerbeer-Liszt	*Réminiscences de Robert le Diable*

RECITAL VI

Chopin	Fantasy in F minor, 6 Preludes, 4 Mazurkas, 4 Ballades, Impromptus, Nos. 2 and 3, Noc turnes in D-flat minor, G major, C minor, Bar carolle, 3 Waltzes Op. 42; Op. 69, No. 1; Op. 34, No. 2, Scherzo No. 1, Sonata No. 2 (Fu neral March), Berceuse, Polonaises in F-sharp minor, C minor, A-flat major

RECITAL VII

Chopin	11 Etudes
Glinka	Tarantella, Barcarolle, *Souvenir de Mazurka* Balakirev Scherzo in B-flat minor, Mazurka in A major, Islamey
Tchaikovsky	*Chant sans paroles*, Op. 2, No. 3, Valse-Scherzo, Romance, Op. 5, *Scherzo à la russe*, Op. 1, No. 1

César Cui	Quasi-Scherzo, Op. 22, No. 4, Polonaise in C major, Op. 22, No. I
Rimsky-Korsakov	Etude, Novelette, Valse
Liadov	Etude in A-flat major, Intermezzo in D major
A. Rubinstein	Sonata in F major, Op. 41, Theme and Varia tions from the C minor Sonata, Op. 20, Scherzo from the A minor Sonata, Op. 100
N. Rubinstein	*Feuillet d'album*, Valse in A-flat major, Op. 16

On June 14th, 1886, the reviewer of the London *Times* wrote of these concerts:

> " Those in his audience who have travelled with him the long way from Couperin and Bach to Liszt and Tchaikovsky may say that the development of piano-forte music is no longer a sealed book to them... It is by tracing this gradual growth through its various phases that Rubinstein has made his recitals so valuable to the students, displaying at the same time his own genius as an executant in the most brilliant light."[7]

During the season of 1886-1887, Rubinstein conducted a series of ten "Historic symphonic concerts" in St. Petersburg, that included compositions from Mozart to Tchaikovsky, Borodin and Balakirev.

In 1887, Anton resumed the directorship of the St. Petersburg Conservatory. As before, he focused his efforts on improving the overall educational process and bringing the young institution to the level of the old and widely respected European conservatories. Apart from his administrative duties, Rubinstein taught many piano students. He donated his whole salary to the Conservatory fund.

In 1887-1888, Rubinstein gave a special course for students of the piano faculty, entitled "The history of Piano Literature", consisting of 58 lectures. As illustrations to these lectures, he performed 1302 compositions by seventy-eight composers. The lecture part of these presentations was no less interesting than the musical demonstrations. He said of Bach:

"Study Bach, look deep into him; let him be your teacher. When dramatic, lyrical and romantic music gets you tired, turn to Bach: in his music you will find delight and consolation. Imagine that on a hot summer's day you are wandering through city streets melted by the sun. You are tired and exhausted. Suddenly you see the old cathedral, blackened with age. Go inside it, and you will find freshness and tranquillity; all your passions will cool down."[8]

Rubinstein's characterization of Beethoven was as follows: "Till now we have known piano music characterized by playfulness and grace (Couperin), grandeur (Bach), amiability and cordiality (Haydn, Mozart). However, we have not found yet in their music either a soul or dramaticism. The person who introduced them in music, was Beethoven."[9] It is interesting to note that, as illustrations in his lectures on Beethoven, Rubinstein performed all the composer's piano sonatas, variations and *Bagatelles*.

The following year, Anton reduced the enormous scope of this course. This time it consisted of thirty-two lectures and was devoted to piano students and teachers, theorists and also musicians not affiliated with the Conservatory. Both courses recieved enthusiastic reception from the media and audiences. César Cui, who wrote down and then published Rubinstein's lectures, pointed out that "a complete picture of the development of piano music was given to the audience from both technical and interpretative perspective."[10]

Upon the completion of the second course, the Conservatory's teachers presented Rubinstein with a silver plate bearing the names of fifty-seven composers whose music he had performed and commented on.

Rubinstein's sixtieth birthday was widely celebrated in Russia in 1889. In St. Petersburg, various festivities lasted for a whole week, from November 17th till November 22nd. For this occasion, Tchaikovsky composed the *a capella* choral piece *Privet Tebe (Greeting to You)*, which was performed on the inaugural evening on November 18th, 1889. Apart from this official ceremony, two special concerts with Tchaikovsky as conductor were given on November 19th and 21st. The programs included various compositions by Rubinstein - *The Russian Symphony*, Op. 107, *Konzert-stück* (with a hero of the day as a soloist), the tone poem *Russia,* and the oratorio *The Tower of Babel.* This last work required the participation of soloists, orchestra and a choir of 700 singers. During the same week Rubinstein's opera *Gorusha* was premiered at the Mariinsky Theatre under the baton of Eduard Nápravnik.

In the late 1880s, Rubinstein was able to realize his idea of establishing an international competition for young pianists and composers. To make this project feasible, he donated 25,000 rubles to a special fund and the interest would go to the competition's winners. According to Rubinstein's desire, such competitions were to be held only once every five years in St. Petersburg, Berlin, Vienna and Paris. The first competition took place in 1890 in St. Petersburg, where its winners were Ferruccio Busoni (composition) and Nicolai Dubasov (piano). These competitions were held regularly until 1910.

In 1891, Tsar Alexander III imposed strict anti-semitic laws, which established quotas for admitting Jews to conservatories and honouring them upon graduation. Rubinstein openly expressed his outrage at these limits and became a target of an anti-semitic campaign in Russian newspapers. This led him to resign once and for all from the St. Petersburg Conservatory which he had founded thirty years before. He wrote:

> "I had done all I could and what had to be done... However, I would like to do much more. In trying to do so, I found serious obstacles, in particular, indifference from those who could help and a hostile attitude on the part of our press towards everything I did. One has to agree that under such circumstances it was difficult to do anything: there was animosity, there was indifference, there were people who did me harm, there were people who oppressed me..."[11]

In 1891, after obtaining a legal divorce from his wife Vera, Rubinstein left Russia and moved to Dresden. In Germany, he devoted his time to composition and taught a few students, including Joseph Hofmann. While residing in Dresden, Anton gave a few charity concert tours through Germany and Austria.

Owing to deteriorating health, he returned to Russia in the summer of 1894. He passed away on November 20th of the same year at his summer retreat in Peterhof near St. Petersburg.

Rubinstein's enormous individuality expressed itself in composing, conducting and piano playing. He was an extremely prolific composer, whose legacy consisted of 14 operas, including *Moses*, Op. 112 and *Christus*, Op. 117, 4 oratorios, one ballet, 6 symphonies, 3 tone poems, 5 concertos for piano, one concerto for violin, two concertos for cello, numerous vocal pieces, piano pieces and piano miniatures. As a composer he did not possess a vivid originality and was under the strong influence of such great romantics as Mendelssohn, Shumann and Liszt. Though many of his compositions enjoyed tremendous popularity during his lifetime and were widely performed both in Russia and abroad, only a few of them are heard today. Among these are his operas *The Demon* and *Die Makkabäer* (*Maccabees*), the piano Concerto No. 4, Op. 70, the vocal cycle *Persian Songs,* and some romances and piano miniatures.

Rubinstein's main achievement lay in the field of piano playing. He was one of the greatest pianists in the history of music and one of the greatest figures of the romantic era of piano playing. Tchaikovsky, who listened to Rubinstein many times, called him 'a genius virtuoso' and 'the tsar of pianists'. Rubinstein possessed a volcanic temper that captivated any audience. His performing style was heroic and poetic at the same time. He was a virtuoso, but merely demonstrating his virtuosity was never his goal. Sometimes, being driven by an eruptive temperament, he could make a few mistakes, but they could never undermine the overall interpretation of the composition.

Rubinstein often told his students: "Do you think that a piano you play on, is a single instrument? No, it is the equivalent of one hundred instruments." Indeed, Rubinstein's piano sounded like a powerful and sensivite orchestra rather than a keyboard instrument.

A few years before his death, the old musician had published an autobiography in which he summed up his life in the following words: "I lived, loved and played."[12]

Although some rudimentary recording technique was available in the 1890s, no records of Rubinstein's are known. However, unanimously enthusiastic descriptions of his performances can be found in the testimonies of such great musicians as Liszt, Mendelssohn, von Bülow, Leschetizky, Tchaikovsky, Paderewski and many others. Rubinstein was a legendary figure for his contemporaries and remains such a figure for us; his art was and remains one of the highest achievements in the history of the piano.

Notes

1.   S. Melnik. *Anton iand Nicolai Rubinsteiny (Anton and Nicolai Rubinsteins)*, Jerusalem, 1990, p. 11

2.   Ibid., p. 12.

3.   Ibid., p. 14.

4.   Ibid., p. 23.

5.   Auer, Leopold, *My Long Life in Music*, F.A. Stokes Co., N.Y., 1923.

6.   S. Melnik, op. cit., p. 58.

7.   Cited in Harvey Sacks, *Virtuoso*, Thames and Hudson, London, 1982, p. 64.

8.   A.G. Rubinstein, *Literaturnoe nasledie* (*Literary Heritage*), Moscow, 1986, p. 158

9.   Ibid., p. 167.

10.   C. Cui, *Istoricheskaya literatura fortepiannoy muziki, lekcii Rubinsteina,1888-1889* (*Historical Piano Litera ture, Rubinstein's Lectures of 1888-1889*), St. Petersburg 1889, p. 4.

11.   A.G. Rubinstein, op. cit., p. 232.

12.   A.G. Rubinstein, *Vospominaniya (1829-1889)*, (*Memoirs 1829-1889*) *Russkaya starina*, November 1889.

2

ADOLF BRODSKY

A SON OF RUSSIA
A STEPSON OF MANCHESTER

AT THE END OF THE 19ᵀᴴ CENTURY and the beginning of the 20th it was North America rather than Great Britain which attracted musicians from continental Europe. Nevertheless, of the few who chose to reside in England was one world class musician - the violinist Adolph Davidovich Brodsky.

Adolph Brodsky
(with wife Anna)

He was born in Taganrog (Russia) in 1851. Brodsky's parents did not have any musical education. However, his mother possessed a good voice and was a fine amateur singer. His father, who had perfect pitch, always tuned Adolph's violin when he was a small boy. Before the age of five, Adolph received his first toy violin as a present from his father and started to play simple melodies by ear. His first teacher was a musician from a local military band who also played the violin.

In 1857, Adolph's mother passed away and the rest of the family moved to Kherson. There was no violin teacher in this small town so Adolph's father took him to Odessa, where the boy studied with the lead violinist of the Opera Theatre's orchestra. Adolph's study with him was irregular because his teacher was given to drink; however, the boy made significant progress. As early as 1860, at the age of eight,

Adolph gave his first public performance at the Odessa Opera Theatre. This concert was to play an important role in Adolph's life. Immediately after the concert, a group of wealthy Odessa residents established a charitable fund to subsidize advanced musical education for the young violinist.

The financial security this fund provided enabled the boy and his father to go to Vienna. On their way to the Austrian capital they made a short stop in Berlin where Adolph played for the composer Giacomo Meyerbeer. The latter was deeply impressed by the young violinist's performance and gave him excellent references.

Upon arrival in Vienna, Adolph was accepted into the Conservatory, where he studied violin with Josef Hellmesberger. Very soon, the new teacher realized how talented his student was and encouraged and supported his musical development. Adolph graduated from the Conservatory in 1866 and in the same year was invited by Hellmesberger to join his Quartet.

In 1868, competing with thirty musicians, he procured the position of violinist with the Imperial Opera House and he also started teaching violin privately.

In 1870, Adolph returned to Russia and embarked upon the career of a concert violinist. He gave numerous performances in Odessa, Kherson, Kiev, Kharkov, many other Ukrainian cities and went on a prolonged concert tour through the Caucasus.

When Ferdinand Laub, the first Professor of violin at the Moscow Conservatory, passed away in 1875, Brodsky took the position of Assistant Professor at this institution. As many other violinists, Adolph was affected by "conductor fever", and during two years, from 1879 till 1881, he conducted the Kiev Symphony Orchestra. On May 13, 1880, he married Anna Skadovska. They were acquainted for many years, and Adolph played the violin quite often at her parents' country estate near Kherson.

Anna's father was a wealthy landowner; both his daughters Anna and Olga, received a comprehensive education at home and graduated from high school. Using their own money, they organized an elementary school for peasant children and worked with great enthusiasm as teachers. Since women were not accepted in Russian universities, the Skadovska sisters went to Paris and there studied natural sciences.

After Anna's marriage, she devoted herself completely to family life and her husband's musical career. In Anna, Adolph found a rare combination of a loving wife, a devoted friend and a wise adviser.

In the winter of 1880, Brodsky went to Paris hoping to give a few recitals and to perform with local symphony orchestras. Here he became a good friend of Camille Saint-Saëns who wanted to help the young Russian musician. They played together in the homes of wealthy patrons of the arts, influential musicians and impresarios. There is some evidence that at one of such musicales, they even performed Tchaikovsky's Violin Concerto in D, Op. 35 composed in 1878.

Despite all the efforts made by Saint-Saëns and Brodsky, the latter was unable to get any engagement in Paris. At least to some extent, this failure was softened by Brodsky's acquaintance with the Russian writer Ivan Turgenieff. They met at Pauline Viardo's house, and both the writer's appearance and his deep intellect impressed Adolph. Turgenieff told him numerous stories of great Russian writers, many of whom he knew personally. Brodsky remembered this meeting for the rest of his life and treasured the postcards and notes he received from Turgenieff in Paris.

In 1881, the Brodskys went to Vienna; Adolph brought the score of Tchaikovsky's Violin Concerto, which still had not been performed publicly. Initially this composition was dedicated to Leopold Auer [1], but he declared it unplayable and did not study it for two years. Tchaikovsky was very disappointed with this lack of progress and often referred to this Concerto as "an unhappy child."

In Vienna, Brodsky was full of the energy and dedication necessary to fulfil his dream of performing the Concerto for the local audience. The violinist was strongly supported by Hans Richter, conductor of the Vienna Philharmonic Orchestra. Despite the strong opposition of the Vienna Philharmonic Committee, which was responsible for programming, Brodsky insisted on including Tchaikovsky's Concerto in the Vienna Philharmonic Orchestra's program.

In his letters to the composer, Brodsky described the premiere of the Violin Concerto in Vienna:

> "From the time when I first saw this score two years ago, it became my dream to perform it publicly. Several times I started to study the Concerto and then gave it up, because my laziness prevailed over my desire to

achieve the goal. You imposed too many difficulties on this composition. Last year, when I was in Paris, I played it to Laroche [2] so badly that he did not get a proper impression on the Concerto, however, he liked it. The trip to Paris, which was very unsuccessful, lent me great energy (usually failures affect me this way, and when I am successful I become weaker). When I returned to Russia, I set out to work vigorously on your Concerto.

What a lovely composition it is! It could be played endlessly, and it would never bore. This is very important if you want to overcome difficulties. When it seemed to me that I knew the Concerto well, I decided to try my fortune in Vienna. At this point, I want to tell you that I am much indebted to you rather than you are indebted to me. Only the desire to be familiar with the new Concerto encouraged Hans Richter and the orchestra to listen to my performance and recognize me as being fit to participate in one of their concerts. To tell the truth, at this Novitaten-Probe your Concerto was not liked, although my performance was approved... Thus, we found the way to Philharmonic concert. I had to be content with only a single rehearsal, and we wasted out time correcting the score, which was replete with typographic errors. Members of the Philharmonic Orchestra decided to accompany me pianissimo because they were afraid the playing any louder would only emphasize their unfamiliarity with the score. As a result, your composition requiring fine nuances both in the accompaniment and in the solo part, lost something. Richter wanted to make some cuts, but I did not agree with him." [3]

The premiere took place on December 4th, 1881 under the baton of Richter. When the performance was over, there was a lot of noise in the hall. Indignant shouts and hisses were overpowered by storms of applause. Brodsky was recalled three times, and the signs of disapproval were not directed at him but rather to the Concerto he performed. Almost all reviews, which appeared the next day in the Viennese newspapers, were harsh. The most critical review published in *The Neue Freie*

Presse, was written by Eduard Hanslick, the prominent arbiter of musical taste in Vienna. In particular, he wrote:

> "The violinist, A. Brodsky, was ill advised to perform this Concerto before the Viennese audience. Of course, the Russian composer Tchaikovsky possesses no commonplace talent, but his talent is too forced, is produces results which are indigestible, non-selective and tasteless. His compositions known to me... are a strange combination of originality and rudeness, of happy thoughts and dreary refinement. This is the case as regards his latest, lengthy and pretentious Violin Concerto. For a while, it is musical and not without inspiration, but soon rudeness gains the upper hand and dominates until the end of the first movement. The violin is not being played but scratched, torn and roared. I do not know whether it is possible to play correctly these hair-raising difficulties, but I do know that trying to reproduce them, Mr. Brodsky tortured his audience no less than he did himself. The Adagio, with its mellow Slavonic melancholy, reconciles us and wins us over. But it ends shortly, making way for a Finale that transports us into the brutal dark gaiety on a Russian church altar Holy Day. We clearly see wild, vulgar faces, hear coarse oaths and smell undistilled vodka. Speaking on sensuous paintings, Friedrich Fisher once said that there were pictures "one could see stinking". Tchaikovsky's Violin Concerto brings us face to face for the first time with the terrible thought: may there not also be compositions which the listener "would find stinking?" [4]

Tchaikovsky was deeply hurt by this review, but, despite it, was very thankful to Brodsky. In a letter to his publisher, Peter Jurgenson, Tchaikovsky wrote:

> "In the matter of Brodsky, should you know his address, please write him that I am deeply touched by his courage. He expressed it when he performed such a difficult and, apparently, unrewarding composition before the prejudiced audience. While Kotek, my closest friend, was afraid and cowardly abolished the perfor-

mance of my Concerto in St. Petersburg... and Auer, to whom the Concerto was dedicated, creates difficulties for me, I have to be touched by and thankful to dear Brodsky who has suffered the invective of the Viennese press due to my person." [5]

Soon the composer sent a letter to Brodsky thanking him for the Concerto performance and expressing his admiration of Brodsky's courage. Tchaikovsky wrote that he was deeply distressed about the fact that the Concerto was not performed publicly for a long time. He compared his attitudes towards this composition with the acute love felt by a mother towards her disabled child.

To express his gratitude to the violinist, the composer changed the Concerto's dedication – starting from the second edition the name of Auer was replaced by that of Brodsky.

Despite the harsh criticism at the Viennese premiere, Brodsky received invitations to perform Tchaikovsky's Violin Concerto in many German and Austrian cities. In the spring of 1882, he gave its premiere in London and in August of the same year performed it for the first time in Moscow. A few years later, Brodsky was given the composer's portrait, which bore the following inscription: "To the re-creator of the Concerto deemed impossible, from the grateful Peter Tchaikovsky." [6]

Time has been the best judge of this Concerto. For many decades now it has remained a cornerstone of a concert violinist's repertoire. Despite the fact that dozens of CDs with this Concerto have already been issued, new CDs with Tchaikovsky's masterpiece appear on the market each year.

After the Moscow premiere, Brodsky went to Leipzig. His goal was to play in one of the most famous European concert halls, the Gewandhaus.

Inspite of all his credentials, Brodsky was asked to play before the Committee of the Gewandhaus Concerts. His performance of the popular Mendelssohn Concerto was so convincing that he received an immediate invitation. For this event, Brodsky selected the Bach Concerto in A minor as a tribute to the composer who lived and died in that city, and the first movement of his dearly loved Tchaikovsky's Concerto.

His rendition of both compositions was so successful that the next day he received an offer to take a professorial position at the Leipzig Conservatory. Brodsky accepted this offer and for the next few years settled in Leipzig.

In the second part of the nineteenth century, Leipzig was one of the largest European musical centers. It housed a reputable Conservatory, the Gewandhaus, a symphony orchestra, a choir, an opera house and numerous musical festivals. Brodsky participated in many of them. At the 1883 festival he performed the Brahms Violin Concerto with the symphony directed by Artur Nikisch. Although this performance was not a premiere, it marked another milestone in Brodsky's career. As a matter of fact, Leipzig was "a citadel" for Wagner and Liszt, but Brahms, who did not share their musical ideas, was not very popular there. Despite this unfriendly environment, Brodsky's performance attended by Liszt himself, was highly acclaimed by the audience and critics alike, and thereafter he was to make regular appearances at the Gewandhaus.

In Leipzig, Brodsky realized an old dream by establishing a string quartet. The debut of the newly formed quartet took place in the Gewandhaus Hall on February 6, 1884. Brodsky invited Brahms to participate in this event and received a postcard from the composer with one sentence written on the back: "Yes, with pleasure. J. Brahms." [7] The programme of the concert included the following compositions: the String Quartet in G, Op. 76, [1] I by Haydn, the Violin Sonata in G, Op. 78 by Brahms and the String Quartet in C sharp minor, Op. 131 by Beethoven. When the Sonata was performed by Brodsky and Brahms, the latter whispered to the page turner Ottokar Nováček who was Brodsky's student: "This fellow does play beautifully, doesn't he?" [8]

During the next several seasons, Brodsky's Quartet gave a series of concerts in the Gewandhaus Hall, which attracted not only the local audience but also numerous foreign listeners from many European countries. Brodsky's programming was typically innovative and included compositions unfamiliar to the audience. In a concert on November 17th, 1888 the Quartet gave the Leipzig premiere of Tchaikovsky's Quartet Op. 30. On April 11th, 1891 they performed the Quintet Op. 111 by J. Brahm for the first time in Leipzig, and during the 1890 season, they premiered the Quintet by Christian Sinding. [9]

During his Leipzig years, Brodsky became acquainted with such musicians as Hans von Bülow, [10] the Griegs, Christian Sinding, Ferruccio Busoni. [11] With some of them, he eventually established a close friendship.

Bülow greatly appreciated Brodsky and his Quartet. As a sign of this appreciation, on December 17th, 1884 he performed the Quintet by Joseph Ruff with Brodsky's Quartet and, as a soloist, the Ruff Piano Sonata. Bülow rejected any fee for his stage appearance.

Soon, Brodsky paid his debt to Bülow. When the latter organized a symphony orchestra in Hamburg in 1888, he was unable to fill a vacancy for the leader. Brodsky, on learning this, immediately offered his services, and for a few months commuted between Leipzig and Hamburg, participating in all the orchestra's rehearsals and concerts. When the season was over, musicians presented Brodsky with a case of fine cigars bearing the following inscription: "To our honoured guest Professor Adolph Brodsky, in kind remembrance of the season 1889-1890, from the members of the Hamburg New Philharmonic Orchestra, conducted by Dr. Hans von Bülow. April, 1889."[12]

Brodsky continued to give concerts and to teach at the Conservatory. Among his students were Hans Becker, who later became a Professor at the Leipzig Conservatory, Ottakar Novàèek, Felix Berber, Alexandr Fidelman,[13] Johan Halvorsen,[14] and Edith Robinson. Novàèek and Fidelman lived in Brodskys' house for several years and were loved by Adolph and by Anna who became a surrogate mother to them.

In the winter of 1887, Tchaikovsky made his first concert tour through Germany as a conductor. He arrived in Leipzig before Christmas. Brodsky met the composer at the railway station and took him home where the Christmas tree had been decorated by Anna, her sister Olga and Olga's son.

Tchaikovsky instantly fascinated his hosts, and the atmosphere of that evening was both entertaining and unpretentious. Tchaikovsky wrote to his brother Modest:

> "I left for Leipzig at 3 o'clock. Brodsky and Siloti met me… There was a supper and a Christmas tree in Brodsky's house. His wife and her sister are charming Russian country women, and all the time I restrained my tears." [15]

The next time Tchaikovsky visited the Brodskys was on December 25, 1887. On this occasion, the Russian composer met Brahms and Grieg for the first time. Tchaikovsky described this meeting in his letter to Modest:

> "Next morning I took a walk…and at dinner time I went to Brodsky together with Siloti. In Brodsky's house there was a rehearsal of the new Trio of Brahms, and Brahms, an insufferable, small, stocky man with a ruddy complexion was very friendly to me… There was also present the charming and pleasant Grieg."[16]

During the next few years, Tchaikovsky visited the Brodskys several times, and each time found understanding, love and caring in their house. Anna Brodsky remembered those visits:

> "Sometimes Tchaikovsky would send us a telegram from Berlin, or any other town where he happened to be, to this effect: "I am coming to see you. Please keep it secret." We knew well what this meant: that he was tired and homesick and in need of friends. Once, after such a telegram, Tchaikovsky arrived just in time for dinner; at first we had him all to ourselves, but after dinner, as he was sitting in the music room with his head leaning on his hand as was his custom, the members of the Brodsky Quartet quietly entered the room, bringing their instruments with them as had been previously arranged. They sat down in silence and played Tchaikovsky's own String Quartet ¹ 3, which they had prepared for a concert. Great was Tchaikovsky's delight! I saw the tears roll down his cheek as he listened, and then, passing from one performer to the other, he expressed his gratitude again and again for the happy hour they had given him. Then turning to Brodsky he said in his naïve way: "I did not know I had composed such a fine quartet. I never liked the finale, but now I see it is really good." [17]

Following Tchaikovsky's invitation, in November 1889, Brodsky's Quartet gave four concerts in Moscow as part of the Russian Musical Society's program.

In his 1891 letter to the Russian composer Julius Conus, Tchaikovsky wrote about Brodsky:

> "He is also a fine artist and the best quartet player I ever heard; even better than Laub, whose performance emphasizes a soloist quality rather than an ensemble player quality." [18]

Edward and Nina Grieg often visited the Brodskys in Leipzig. During one such visit, Edward brought a manuscript of his Sonata [1] 3, Op. 45 for violin and piano. He was not satisfied with this composition and wanted to play it with Brodsky. Adolph instantly fell in love with the new Sonata and used all his eloquence to convince Grieg to perform it publicly. They performed the Sonata's premiere December 1887 in the Gewandhaus Hall, and this premiere was a success. Ten years later, while visiting Brodsky in Manchester, Grieg presented him with an inscribed manuscript on the Sonata's violin part. In 1906 Brodsky, together with his wife, a niece and two students were guests of the Griegs and spent three days in Bergen and in Troldhaugen with them. When Brodsky learned of Grieg's death on September 4, 1907, he took a steamer to Bergen and played at his friend's funeral.

In 1890 Anna, Adolph and his pupil Fidelman left for New York, where Brodsky took a position as leader of the New York Symphony Orchestra. The New World disappointed him. Many years later Anna wrote:

> "He daily met with musicians of a type quite new to him, a type which could only have been developed in a country where there was no tradition of serving art for art's sake. He soon saw that money was everything in America, the universal centre of gravity. Even the talent of musicians was measured by the money they earned, and the true love of art seemed very rare. He received an equally unfavourable impression of the music in which he took part: there was always more quantity than quality." [19]

Brodsky was not satisfied with the Orchestra's programming. He felt that annual marathon tours through the USA and Canada were too exhausting. Adolph found more satisfaction playing with the Quartet he formed in New York. Although chamber music was not popular in the city, the Quartet found its niche in its musical life and won the respect of the local audience.

Brodsky's relationship with the New York Symphony's conductor, Walter Damrosch, was far from cloudless. Adolph vigorously defended musicians' rights and insisted on the strict fulfillment of contracts, while Damrosch, being not only a conductor but also a co-owner of the Orchestra, quite often violated them. As a result of one of these "labour disputes" Brodsky quit the New York Symphony and returned to Germany in 1895. Shortly afterwards, he received an invitation from Sir Charles Halle [20] to take a position as leader of his Orchestra along with the professorship at the Royal Manchester College of Music. Almost simultaneously Adolph received offers from conservatories of St. Petersburg, Berlin and Cologne. In spite of Anna's hesitation and worries, Adolph chose England, and the family moved to Manchester.

At the end of 1895 Sir Halle passed away, and Brodsky replaced him as a Director of the Royal Manchester College of Music, remaining in this post till his own death in 1929. Under Brodsky's directorship, the College became one of the best musical institutions in England. Due to his international reputation, Adolph was able to staff the College with such outstanding musicians as Wilhelm Backhaus,[21] Egon Petri,[22] Carl Fuchs, [23] and his former pupil Arthur Catterall.[24]

Brodsky himself successfully combined directorship and teaching for more than thirty years. Among his students, apart from the mentioned above Catterall, were Anton Maaskoff, Lena Kontorovich, Philip Hecht, Alfred Barker, and Naum Blinder.[25] Many years later, Blinder became a teacher of Isaac Stern, making Brodsky, in a sense, "the musical grandfather" of the famous American violinist.

Mainly due to Brodsky's prestige in the international musical community, the Royal Manchester College of Music attracted students not only from Britain, but from the Continent of Europe and even from the USA. In recognition of his tremendous contribution to the musical life of the city, the University of Manchester awarded Brodsky an honorary Doctoral degree in music in 1902.

In 1899, the old friend of Adolph, Hans Richter was appointed as conductor of the Halle Orchestra, retaining the position until 1911. During that time, very rewarding relationships developed between

Brodsky, Richter and the Orchestra. Many of Brodsky's graduates joined the Orchestra; Brodsky himself played regularly with the Halle Orchestra as a soloist. To commemorate the anniversary of the Tchaikovsky Violin Concerto's premiere in Vienna twenty years earlier, Brodsky performed it in Manchester on December 4th, 1902. As it was in Vienna, Hans Richter was conductor at this performance.

Quite often, Brodsky performed chamber music with such outstanding musicians as the former Liszt's pupil Arthur Friedheim and Busoni. However, Brodsky's "most beloved child" was the quartet he established soon after his arrival in Manchester.

The quartet's regular concerts attracted large audiences and received enthusiastic reviews. Besides Manchester, the quartet toured to other British and Western European cities.

A fruitful collaboration was established between Brodsky's Quartet and the English composer Edward Elgar. Elgar's String Quartet Op. 83 was composed for and dedicated to Brodsky's Quartet. Adolph was one of the best interpreters of Elgar's Violin Concerto and he performed it many times in England and in other European countries. On January 5, 1914 the violinist gave its Vienna premiere. In Brodsky's archives, there is a picture of the composer with his inscription: "To my dear A. and A. Brodskys – Edward Elgar." [26]

In 1921, Brodsky stopped giving public performances. At his farewell concert, given on January 13th, 1921, Adolph performed the same program which he had delivered twenty five years earlier at his first concert in Manchester. It included Bach's A minor Concerto, Tchaikovsky's *Sérenade mélancholique* [27] and Novàèek's *Perpetuum mobile*.

The music critic of *The Manchester Guardian*, Samuel Langford, wrote on this concert:

> "He has preserved throughout his long life, as few musicians have done, the impression that his life has been devoted to the great classical composers and to the timeless elements in his art. That is why he can lay down his bow with a certain grandeur and austerity which make him one with the composers themselves."[28]

In 1921, Anna suffered a massive stroke which left her almost completely disabled. She was bound to a wheelchair, and from then on was entirely restricted to her home. Brodsky did all he could for his wife. At the end of each working day at the College, he devoted the evening hours to Anna reading her books and newspapers and sharing local musical news with her. He not only entertained Anna, but also performed various duties as a nurse.

The situation improved in 1924, when, through Adolph's tremendous efforts, Anna's sister Olga and her son Leon arrived in Manchester from the Soviet Russia. Olga took care of Anna, and Adolph was able to resume, to some extent, his concert activity. He played again with his Quartet and broadcast a few programs as a soloist.

In January 1927, the seventy-six year old Brodsky performed Elgar's Violin Concerto at a concert dedicated to the seventieth anniversary of the composer with Elgar himself conducting the Halle Orchestra. The critic Samuel Langford wrote in *The Manchester Guardian* of this event:

> "Sir Edward Elgar himself seemed more to indulge the orchestra than to rule it; as though he himself was savouring the delight of hearing the most lovely touches of the music given leisurely on beautiful instruments by first-rate players. Dr. Brodsky sought his strength in the expressive features of the work and played them with so much depth of feeling that the question of whether he played all the bravura passages with the strength of a player in his prime never seemed to matter."[29]

Brodsky's last performance with his Quartet took place five weeks before his death which occurred on January 22, 1929. In memory of Brodsky, the Halle Orchestra, under the baton of Sir Hamilton Harty, performed the 'Trauermarsch' from Wagner's *Götterdämmerung*. During this performance three thousand listeners stood on their feet paying tribute to the musician who did so much for the development of musical life in Manchester.

Both Adolph and Anna felt a true love and affection for Manchester, its residents and their numerous friends. In her memoirs, Anna wrote:

> "There are many excellent people all over the world, but to find, as in Manchester, so many attractive and kind and good, residing in one and the same place, was a unique experience for us. Our Manchester friends have helped to strengthen my belief in the essential goodness of humanity, and for that alone I shall always feel deeply indebted to them."[30]

Unfortunately, Brodsky did not make any records. According to reviewers, he possessed solid technique, however, he was not a virtuoso-type violinist. The characteristic features of Brodsky's talent were in-depth musicality and sincerity. He also had a special taste for unknown compositions and boldly included them in his programs.

It is said that quartet music is the most perfect and pure form of musical expression. Brodsky's achievements in this field are enormous. Starting form his youth, he propagated quartet music and brought it to

the audiences in Vienna, Leipzig, New York, Manchester and to many other cities. The tradition of playing quartet music established by him is still alive in Manchester where the "New Brodsky Quartet" consisting of young musicians was formed a few years ago.

Anna survived Adolph by a few months only; she passed away on October 2, 1929. After her death, her sister Olga and her son Leon Picard continued to live in the Brodsky's house. Olga passed away at the age of almost one hundred. After her death, Leon, who never married, secluded himself, and by the end of his life the huge house fell into a state of neglect. Leon died in 1959, and the house passed into the hands of the local Municipality. The decision was made to renovate the house. This necessitated the disposal of its contents which were considered only fit for refuse collection.

Members of the Royal College of Music, learning of this, made a visit to the former Brodsky residence. The scene before them was one of absolute desolation. The place was a shambles. Letters from famous musicians, posters and programs advertising past concerts lay strewn on the floor amidst food leftovers and mousedroppings. Everywhere was invaluable historical details of a priceless musical past destined, all of it, to be destroyed. The College members carefully collected all the material and took it to the College Library. In this way, the valuable Brodsky's archives were saved.

Today, the Brodsky Archives consist of letters to Brodsky from Tchaikovsky, the Griegs, Brahms, Hans von Bülow, Hans Richter, Busoni, Saint-Saⱬns, Edouard Lalo, Théophile Ysaÿe, Elgar and Tourgenieff. It also contains numerous postcards, photos and pictures. Some of the pictures are of special value, such as those with inscriptions from Tchaikovsky, Brahms, Grieg and Elgar. Besides these, the Brodsky collection includes scores, violinist's diplomas, press-clippings, programs and even tickets for his concerts.[31] All this material is being catalogued electronically by archivists of the Royal Northern College of Music Library. Music lovers as well as musicologists in England and many other countries are looking forward to seeing this tremendous work compiled in the near future.

Notes

1. Auer, Leopold (Leo) (1845-1930), a violinist, teacher. Following Anton Rubinstein's invitation in 1868, Auer became a Professor at the St. Petersburg Conservatory and kept this position until 1917. He played first violin in the Russian Musical Society (RMS) Quartet, conducted the RMS Symphony Orchestra, was a soloist of the Mariinski Theatre Orchestra and soloist to His Majesty the Russian Emperor. Violin Concertos by Glazunov and Arensky as well as the Concert Suite by Taneev and *Serénade mélancholique* by Tchaikovsky were dedicated to Auer. Among his students were Jascha Heifetz, Efim Zimbalist, Mischa Elman and Nathan Milstein. In 1917, Auer emigrated to Norway and then to the USA, where he taught at the New York Institute of Musical Art and in the Philadelphia Curtis Institute.

2. Larosche, Herman, (1845-1904), the Russian music critic and musicologist. He published several works on Glinka and Tchaikovsky.

3. Tchaikovsky, Modest, *Zhizn' Petra Il'icha Tchaikovskogo (The Life of Pyotr Ilych Tchaikovsky)*, Vol. II., Moscow, Algorhythm Publishing House, 1997, pp. 427-428.

4. Ibid., pp. 428-429. Friedrich Fisher (1807-1887) referred to in this letter, was a German poet and aesthete.

5. Ibid., p.430.

6. Brodsy, Anna, *A Recollection of a Russian Home,* Second Edition, London, Sherrat and Hughes, 1914, pp. 132-133

7. Ibid., pp. 148.

8. Ibid., p 149.

9. Sinding, Christian, (1856-1941), a Norwegian composer and pianist. Among his compositions are four symphonies three concertos for violin, one concerto for piano, the concerto for strings, more than 200 songs and numerous piano miniatures.

10. Bülow, Hans von, (1830-1894), a German conductor and pianist. He studied piano with Friedrich Wieck and Liszt and gave his first concert tour through Germany in 1853. In 1855-1864 Bülow was a piano Professor at the Berlin Conservatory during which time he developed conducting opportunities in addition to making tours as a concert pianist. As chief conductor of the Munich Royal Opera, he gave the first performance of Wagner's *Tristan and Isolde* (1865) and *Die Meistersinger von Nürnberg* (1868). In 1880 he became the court conductor to the Duke of Meiningen and made this court orchestra the best in Europe. In 1888, Bülow became conductor of the opera and orchestra in Hamburg. He composed orchestral and piano works and published his own edition of Beethoven's Piano Sonatas.

11. Busoni, Ferruccio, (1866-1924), the Italian composer, conductor and pianist. He taught in Helsinki (1889), Moscow (1890) and Boston (1891-1894). As a pianist, he gave concerts around the world. Among his compositions are several operas, several concertos for piano and violin, chamber music, music for piano. Busoni made numerous piano transcriptions of compositions by Bach, Beethoven, Chopin, Mozart, Schubert, Liszt, Wagner and Schoenberg.

12. Brodsky, Anna, op. cit., pp. 155-156.

13. Fidelman, Alexandr (Ruvim), a violinist and teacher. He studied violin with Brodsky in Leipzig and with Auer in St. Petersburg. He taught at the RMS College in Odessa where his students were Mischa Elman, Naum Blinder, Yakov Magaziner, and Naum Skomorovsky. In 1907, Fidelman went to Berlin and continued to teach. He also gave concerts around the world.

14. Halvorsen, Johan, (1864-1935), a Norwegian conductor, composer, violinist. He studied violin with Auer and Brodsky. In 1899-1929 he was a principal conductor of the National Theatre's Symphony Orchestra in Christiania (Oslo). As a violinist, Halvorsen gave concerts in Norway and other countries. Among his compositions are three symphonies, nine orchestral suites, vocal and incidental music.

15.   Tchaikovsky, Modest, Vol. III, op. cit., p. 181.

16.   Ibid., pp. 181-182.

17.   Brodsky, Anna, op. cit., p. 170.

18.   Tchaikovsky, Modest, Vol. III, op. cit.,p. 432.

19.   Ibid., pp. 188-189.

20.   Hallé, Charles, (1819-1895), a German pianist and conduc-
        tor. He went to Paris in 1836, becoming a friend of Chopin,
        Liszt, and Berlioz. Halle settled in Manchester in 1848. He
        was the first pianist to play all Beethoven's piano Sonatas in
        Manchester, London and Paris. In Manchester, he founded the
        choral society and the symphony orchestra; he also established
        a series of chamber and orchestral concerts. Halle conducted
        opera seasons in Manchester and London and was a Director
        of the Bristol Music Festival in 1873-1893.

21.   Backhaus, Wilhelm , (1884-1969), a German pianist. He stu-
        died piano with Eugene d'Albert and made his concert debut at
        the age of 16. Backhaus concertized around the world and was
        considered as one of the best interpreters of Beethoven and
        Brahms compositions. He was a Professor at the Royal
        Manchester College of Music in 1905.

22.   Petri, Egon, (1881-1962), a Dutch pianist. He studied piano
        with Teresa Carreño and Busoni, and later made concerts in
        many countries. He was a Professor at the Royal Manchester
        College of Music (1906-1910), at the Berlin Hochschule für
        Musik (1921-1925) and at various Ameri-can Universities
        (1940-1957). Petri returned to Europe in 1957 and taught in
        Basel. He was well known as an interpreter of Liszt and Busoni.

23.   Fuchs, Carl, (1865-1951), a German cellist. He studied cello
        in Frankfurt and St. Petersburg (with Karl Davidoff). He was
        lead of the Halle Orchestra in Manchester (1887-1914), a
        Professor at the Royal Manchester College of Music (1893-
        1914 and 1921-1942), and a member of the Brodsky Quartet
        (1895-1926). He puclished memoirs on the Manchester mus-

ical life and the Brodsky Quartet (Fuchs, Carl, *Erinnerunger-eines Offenbacher Cellisten: Musical and Other Recollection*, Manchester: Sherrat and Hughes, 1937.)

24.   Catterall, Arthur, (1883-1943), an English violinist, a pupil of Brodsky. As a soloist, he first played with the Halle Orches tra in 1900. He was leader of many English orchestras and a Professor at the Royal Manchester College of Music (1910-1929). He was also a founder of his own string quartet (1911-1925).

25.   Blinder, Naum, (1889-1965), a violinist and teacher. He stud ied violin with Fidelman in Odessa and with Brodsky in Man chester. In 1932, he moved to the USA and became leader of the San-Francisco Symphony Orchestra. Among his students were Isaac Stern and Glenn Dicterow.

26.   Knowles, Clifford, "Brodsky in Manchester, Part I," *Music Mat ter* 21, 1986, p. 5 (thereafter Clifford Knowless). The writer would like to thank Mrs. Helen Smith of the Royal Northern College of Music Library for providing a copy of this article.

27.   It is interesting to note that similar to the Violin Concerto, the *Sérenade mélancholique* by Tchaikovsky, though dedicated to Auer, was premiered by A. Brodsky in 1875.

28.   Clifford Knowles, Part II, op. cit., p. 5.

29.   Ibid., p. 6.

30.   Brodsky, Anna, op. cit., pp. 206-208.

31.   For more on Brodsky's Collection see: Geoffrey Thomason., "The Brodsky Archive at the RNCN," *Brio*, 22, 1985, pp. 46-49. The writer would like to thank Mrs. Helen Smith of the Royal Northern College of Music Library for providing a copy of this article.

A REMARKABLE WOMAN

ROSALIA PASTERNAK HAS REMAINED in the shadow of her husband, the artist Leonid Pasternak,[1] and of her elder son Boris, the Russian poet and novelist.[2] But such an extraordinary person and outstanding musician merits special consideration and appreciation. She was born in Odessa on 7 February, 1867, into a relatively prosperous Jewish family. Her father, Isidor Kaufman, owned a small mineral water factory, while her mother, Bertha, was a devoted housewife.

Rosalia was a *wunderkind.* She began to play the piano at the age

Rosalia Pasternak
The Pasternak family in 1901: left to right (Boris, Leonid, Rosalia, Nurse, Zhosefina)

of five; at the age of eight, she gave her first public performance. From 1878 until 1882 she studied with the internationally known pianist and composer Ignace Tedesco.[3] In 1880-1, she made two extensive concert tours in southern Russia, and the performances she gave in Poltava, Kharkov and, especially, Kiev were received with great enthusiasm.[4] In the winter of 1881, at the invitation of Anton Rubinstein, she gave concerts in Moscow and St. Petersburg. The famous pianist attended Rosalia's rehearsal of one of Chopin's piano concertos in St. Petersburg. When she had finished, the maestro rushed on to the stage, embraced her, lifted her up on to the piano and exclaimed: "That is how it should be played!"[5]

In St. Petersburg Rosalia also performed chamber music together with the great Spanish violin virtuoso Pablo Sarasate and the brilliant Russian cellist Karl Davidov.[6]

Following Rubinstein's advice, Rosa went to Vienna, where she studied with the most distinguished piano teacher of the late nineteenth century, Theodor Leschetizky, whose pupils Mieczyslaw Horszowski, Ignace Paderewski, Benno Moiseiwitsch, Ignace Friedman and Artur Schnabel. In Vienna, the young pianist gave several recitals which received highly favourable reviews from leading music critics. Rosa's piano career was so remarkable that a monograph on her achievements in performance was published as early as 1885.[7]

Rosalia returned to Odessa in 1887 and immediately took a professorial position at the local branch of the Imperial Russian Music Society. On holiday in Odessa in 1885, she had become acquainted with the young and promising artist Leonid Pasternak. They were married in Moscow on 14 February, 1889. In April of that year Rosalia quit her job and she and her husband moved to Moscow.

In 1890, Rosalia gave birth to her son Boris and in 1893 her second son Aleksander[8] was born. Many years later Aleksander recalled:

> "She was the kindest person and she devoted all her energy and temperament to her complicated, and sometimes controversial, family life and her husband's artistic career in order to make them both move smoothly. Thanks to her efforts, father was released from routine family duties and spent his entire time painting either us or other sitters... Mother acted as a secretary and participated in his business affairs, correspondence and negotiations. He was released from everything that could worry him. The only worry he was allowed to have, and which he needed, was the creative one... And when she had done everything she could, when everything was on the right track and she could take a rest, she was transformed immediately from the family's engine driver...into a fine pianist immersed in the world of emotions...and the nocturnes and ballades of Chopin."[9]

In the Pasternaks' Moscow flat, the old Russian tradition of informal musical soirées was revived. Among those who participated in the improvised domestic concerts were prominent musicians such as Anatoly Brandukov,[10] Alfred von Glehn,[11] Modest Altshuler,[12] Ivan Hrimalý,[13] Aleksander Mogilevsky,[14] Mikhail Bukinik[15] and David Shor.[16] Very often they would sit around until late evening, playing and discussing their favourite music.

One such gathering, on 23 November, 1894, was attended by the novelist Leo Tolstoy and his daughters Tatyana and Maria. They came to hear Tchaikovsky's Piano Trio in A minor *"In Memory of a Great Artist"*, which Rosalia, Hrimalý and Brandukov performed in memory of the recently deceased Rubinstein and the artist Nikolai Gue, a close friend of Tolstoy. Almost one year earlier the same musicians had played this Trio in the Moscow Hall of Columns of the Nobility Assembly in memory of Tchaikovsky, who had died in St. Petersburg in October 1893. Many Moscow newspapers published enthusiastic reviews of this performance, pointing out Rosalia Pasternak's beautiful rendition of the piano part.

In March 1895, Rosalia, Hrimalý and Altshuler performed a Trio by Rubinstein at a charity concert for students of the School of Painting, Sculpture and Architecture. In his review, the leading Moscow critic Nikolai Kashkin, a professor at the Moscow Conservatory, praised the musicians and, in particular, expressed the hope that Rosalia's performing career would continue.

It seemed that the critic's hopes were to be realized. In October 1893, Rosalia played Schumann's Piano Quintet in E-flat major, Op. 44, and on 19 November, 1895, she performed *The Death of Isolde* (Wagner-Liszt) in the Hall of Columns. A few minutes before her November stage appearance, Rosalia was informed that both her sons had fallen seriously ill with fever. Rushing home immediately after the performance, she made a pledge to end her concert career if the boys recovered. Several days later Boris and Aleksander made a complete recovery. Rosalia did not play publicly for the next twelve years. There may have been other reasons, including the state of her own health, which contributed to such a dramatic turn in her life.

The Pasternak family was also growing. A daughter, Zhosefina,[17] was born in 1900 and Lydia[18] arrived in 1902.

In the summer of 1903 the family took their holidays in Obolenskoye near Moscow, where Aleksander Scriabin was their neighbour. At that time, the composer was working tirelessly on his Symphony No. 3 in C major. Hiding in the bushes near Scriabin's cottage, Boris and Aleksander listened for hours to this ecstatic, mercurial music as it was being composed.

The families became acquainted and visited each other often. Scriabin, himself a brilliant pianist, brought his new piano pieces to Rosalia and asked her to play them for him. The friendship between the two musicians continued in Moscow, where Scriabin and his wife often visited the Pasternaks home.

In the autumn of 1905 political unrest spread throughout Russia. Life in the capital became so dangerous that the Pasternaks decided to leave the city and move to Germany. They settled in Berlin, where Leonid resumed his painting.

Now living away from Moscow and free of routine domestic obligations, Rosalia expressed a revived interest in a concert career and began to practise daily.

Immediately following her return to Moscow in 1906, she began preparing programmes. From 1907 onwards, she often played publicly either as a soloist or a member of chamber ensembles. Unfortunately, no complete list of her stage appearances has survived and only a few of them are known. On 14 March, 1907, she played at a charity gala concert given by prominent Moscow musicians and actors. Two weeks later she gave a recital.

On 26 February, 1908, the outstanding Moscow musicologist Yuly Engel gave a public lecture entitled "Romanticism in music". His presentation was accompanied by a concert in which Rosalia performed works by Chopin and Schumann and, together with Mogilevsky and Bukinik, Trios by Schubert and Mendelssohn.

On October 3rd, 1908, Rosalia and Mogilevsky played sonatas for violin and piano in the Small Hall of Nobility Assembly. The programme included the Sonata in G major, op. 96 by Beethoven, the Sonata in C minor by Aleksander Vinkler[19] (its Moscow première), and the Sonata in A major by César Franck. An enthusiastic review of this concert by Engel appeared in the Moscow newspaper *Russkiye vedomosti*. Both musicians performed Vinkler's sonata once again at a matinée in the Hall of Columns on 11 January, 1909.

The Pasternaks were, for many years, close friends of Leo Tolstoy. Leonid visited him often both in Moscow and at his Yasnaya Polyana estate and made many pictures, drawings and sketches of the great writer. The last time Leonid went to Yasnaya Polyana, on April 30th, 1909, he was accompanied by his wife and Mogilevsky, who played for Tolstoy and his household. The memory of this performance, as well as of several earlier ones, was kept alive in the family for many years. In 1912, after Tolstoy's death, his daughter Tatyana wrote to a relative: "Please give my regards to the Pasternaks. They are both great artists, and father would often shed tears when he heard her playing."[20]

In commemoration of the first anniversary of Tolstoy's death, a concert, organized by Sergei Koussevitsky, was held in the Great Hall of the Moscow Conservatory. The core of the programme comprised two of Tolstoy's favourite compositions, Beethoven's Fifth Symphony and the Tchaikovsky Piano Trio. The latter was performed by Rosalia, David Kreyn[21] and David Zisserman.[22] Aleksander Pasternak, who was waiting for his mother back stage, recalls:

> "I was listening to very familiar music but I could not recognize it due to its new meaning. I had never heard such an interpretation before. It seemed to me that it was being performed not by my mother but by someone else... I noticed Koussevitsky standing near the stage door, which was ajar. He was motionless. His head was bent in his usual pose... As a conductor, he listened to the ensemble with rapt attention... Suddenly he winced, trembled and passed his hand over his eyes, brushing away a tear."[23]

This was Rosalia's last concert performance. In 1914 she played in a few charity concerts in honour of wounded Russian officers, but these were of limited artistic value. While she continued to play at domestic gatherings, they became rarer as the war dragged on.

Following the October 1917 Revolution, living conditions in Moscow deteriorated drastically. There were severe food and fuel shortages and public services were either significantly reduced or cut completely. The Pasternaks were unable to obtain the medical care they required and, on those grounds, applied for an exit visa. In the autumn of 1921, with the permission of the Soviet authorities, Leonid Pasternak, his wife and his two daughters left Russia and went to Germany for a second time. In Berlin, Rosalia helped her husband in many ways, managing his correspondence, negotiating with clients and sponsors and organizing exhibitions. Gradually Leonid Pasternak became a well established painter with a steady income. In 1922 and 1927 he held successful exhibitions in Berlin and in 1932 the first monograph on his artistic achievements appeared.[24]

After 1933, following the Nazi accession to power, the Pasternaks' life in Germany became increasingly difficult. With the proclamation of anti-semitic laws, Leonid was prohibited from painting and teaching and the typesetting for his new album was deliberately destroyed.

In 1938, the Pasternaks moved to England, where their daughters had settled earlier. In London on 23 August, 1939, Rosalia died of a heart attack.

Two months before her death Rosalia played her favourite Schumann Quintet. Leonid wrote in his diary: "Just as a flickering candle flares brightly for the last time only to go out in the next moment, forever... so with my wife."[25]

Unfortunately, Rosalia did not make any records and any evaluation of her playing must, therefore, be based on scant information from memoirs and reviews. It would appear that she possessed a technique which provided her with complete freedom of expression. Her singing tone, the hallmark of Leschetizky's teaching, was remarkable for its pure beauty, her phrasing was expressive and perfectly chiselled. Her style on stage was unpretentious: she avoided excessive gestures and body movements.

Rosalia played almost all of Chopin's works. Another Romantic whom Rosalia took to heart was Schumann and she loved to perform his *Carnaval, Kreisleriana* and Sonata in G minor. She also played piano sonatas by Scarlatti, Mozart and Beethoven and several of Mozart's piano concertos. Her immense chamber-music repertoire included sonatas for violin and piano by Mozart, Beethoven, Franck and Grieg, trios by Schubert, Mendelssohn, Rubinstein and Tchaikovsky, quintets by Schubert and Schumann and Schubert's Fantasia in F minor. She did not limit herself to the standard nineteenth-century repertoire, but per-

formed works by contemporaries such as Scriabin, Johan Svendsen[26] and
Aleksander Vinkler.

Rosalia Pasternak's concert career was relatively brief but distinguished, nonetheless. Yet her place in Russian culture should not be
limited to music. For fifty years she was an irreplaceable assistant to her
husband Leonid. She also revealed to him the world of classical music
and brought him into the circle of refined musicians. Leonid remembered: "I did not understand the music of the old masters and it was
only thanks to my wife that I began to value and appreciate it... I had
never read any theoretical books on music, nor did I know a single note.
Yet I was able to understand the essence of symphonies."[27]

Under his wife's influence, Leonid created a fascinating portrait gallery of outstanding musicians, including Rubinstein, Tchaikovsky,
Scriabin, Rachmaninoff, Prokofiev, Chaliapin, Koussevitsky, Godowsky,
Hofmann, Landowska and Nikisch and towering figures from the past
such as Bach, Beethoven and Mendelssohn.

Rosalia herself and her son Boris, who began his creative career as a
composer, were among the artist's favourite subjects and he painted them
frequently. Many of his drawings and sketches of them possess a dis-
tinctive "musical" flavour.

Rosalia had considerable influence on Boris, too. The music of
Chopin, which his mother loved and played so often, accompanied him
from his infancy and become part of his life. According to the Russian
musicologist Boris Katz, "for Pasternak, Chopin was not a subject of
musical contemplation...but 'a life-time interlocutor'."[28] It is interesting
to note that in 1945, Boris Pasternak published an essay on Chopin
which presented an unconventional musicological and philosophical analysis of his piano works.[29] Under the initial influence of Rosalia and
Scriabin, and thanks to his long friendship with such outstanding musicians as Heinrich Neuhaus, Maria Yudina and Sviatoslav Richter, music
became an important element of Boris Pasternak's creative works. Many
of his poems use musical images, including *Improvisation* (1916), *Defi-
nition of Creativity* (1917), *Wedding* (1954) and *In Everything I want
to Reach* (1956), in which he wrote:

> " I should have mint and roses
> Breathingthere -
> Sedge, meadows, haymaking,
> And thundrous air;

So Chopin once enclosed
The plenitude
Of farmsteads, parks, groves, graves
In his *Études*.

The torment and delight
Of triumph so
Achieved tightens the bowstring,
Bending the bow."[30]

Notes:

1.   Pasternak, Leonid, (1862-1945), painter and teacher, professor at the Moscow School of Painting, Sculpture and Architecture (1894-1921); illustrated Tolstoy's *War and Peace* and *Resurrection.* His greatest achievement was a portrait gallery of distinguished Russian and European writers, poets, musicians, philosophers, scientists and politicians, including Maksim Gorky, Valery Brusov, Vsevolod Ivanov, Konstantin Balmont, Rainer-Maria Rilke, Emil Verhaern, Anton Rubinstein, Sergei Rachmaninoff, Aleksander Scriabin, Sergei Prokofiev, Lev Shestov, Albert Einstein and Ilya Mechnkov.

2.   Pasternak, Boris, (1890-1960), poet, novelist and translator; Nobel Prize winner in 1958.

3.   Tedesco, Ignace, (1817-1882), Czech pianist, composer, conductor and teacher; moved to Odessa in 1840; played extensively in concerts in Russia and Europe.

4.   For further details on Rosalia's early performing career see Serge Levitsky, "Rose Koffman-Pasternak: la mère du poète"("Rose Koffman-Pasternak: The Poet's Mother") *Etudes Slaves et Est-Europèennes,* no. 8, 1963, 73-80.

5.   *"Raskat improvizatsiy"...Muzika v tvorchestve, sud'be i v dome Pasternaka ("The Thunder of Improvisations"...Music in Pasternak's Creative Work, Life and Home).* Edited by Boris Katz. Sovetskiy Kompozitor, Leningrad, 1991, p. 243 (hereafter *Raskat*).

6.   Davidov, Karl, (1838-1889), cellist, conductor, composer and teacher, performed with Rubinstein, Sergei Taneev and Liszt, was professor at the St. Petersburg Conservatory in 1862-87 and its director in 1876-87

7.   Bachmann, O., *Rosa Kaufmann: Eine biographische Skizze, nebst Auszug einiger Rezensionen (A Biographical Sketch Along with a Selection of a Few Reviews).* Odessa, L. Nitzsche, 1885.

8.   Pasternak, Aleksander, (1893-1982), architect, teacher, memoirist.

9.   *Raskat,* op. cit., pp. 85-86.

10.   Anatoly, Brandukov, (1856-1930), cellist and teacher, in 1878-1906 lived mainly abroad and performed with Liszt and Rubinstein; director of Moscow Philharmonic Society's College of Music from 1906; professor at the Moscow Conservatory from 1921.

11.   Glehn von, Alferd, (1858-1927), cellist and teacher, professor at the Moscow Conservatory from 1890; emigrated to Estonia in 1921 and Germany in 1925.

12.   Altshuler, Modest, (1873-1963), cellist and conductor, member of the Moscow Trio; emigrated to the USA in 1898, where he performed for the first time many of Scriabin's compositions.

13.   Ivan Hrimalý (1844-1915), violinist and teacher; graduated from the Prague Conservatory in 1861 and became a professor at the Moscow Conservatory in 1874, was a member of the Imperial Russian Music Society's Quartet and composed for violin.

14.   Mogilevsky, Aleksander, (1885-1955), violinist and teacher; professor at the Moscow College of Music from 1910 and Moscow Conservatory from 1920; emigrated from Russia in 1922, played in concert throughout the world and eventually settled in Japan, becoming a professor at the Tokyo Conservatory in 1937.

15.   Bukinik, Mikhail, (1872-1947), cellist and teacher; graduated from the Moscow Conservatory in 1895, then played with Sergei Taneev, Konstantin Igumnov and Wanda Landowska; professor at the Kharkov Conservatory in 1919-1922; emigrated to the USA in 1922; composed and made numerous transcriptions for cello.

16.   Shor, David, (1867-1942), pianist, teacher and lecturer; founding member of the Moscow Trio; became a professor at the Moscow Conservatory in 1919; emigrated to Palestine in 1927.

17. Pasternak, Zhosefina, (1900-1993), philosopher and poet; after father's death put his archives in order and prepared his *Zapisiraznykh let* (*Notes from Various Years*) for publication (see note 27).

18. Pasternak-Slater, Lydia, (1902-1989), biochemist and translator of poetry of Boris Pasternak.

19. Vinkler, Aleksander, (1865-1935), pianist and composer; professor at the St. Peterburg Conservatory 1909-24; emigrated to France in 1925.

20. *Raskat*, op. cit., p. 208.

21. Kreyn, David, (1869-1926), violinist and teacher, member of the Moscow Trio 1894-1926; professor at the Moscow Conservatory.

22. Zisserman, David, (1896-1961), cellist and teacher.

23. *Raskat*, op. cit., p. 187.

24. Osborn, Max, *Leonid Pasternak,* Warsaw, Stybel, 1932.

25. *The Memoirs of Leonid Pasternak,* Translated by J. Bradshaw, with an Introduction by J. Pasternak, Quarter Books, London, Melbourne, New York, 1982, p.77.

26. Svendsen, Johan, (1840-1911), Norwegian composer, conductor and pianist, from 1883 a court conductor in Copenhagen; compositions include two symphonies, violin and cello concertos, chamber music and songs.

27. Pasternak, Leonid, *Zapisi raznykh let* (*Notes from Various Years*), Sovetskiy Khudozhnik, Moscow, 1975, p. 102.

28. *Raskat*, op. cit., pp. 26-27.

29. Ibid, pp. 96-99.

30. Pasternak, Boris, *Selected Poems*, translated from Russian by Jon Stallworthy and Peter France, Penguin Books, London, 1983.

4

WANDA LANDOWSKA

DISCOVERER OF
FORGOTTEN MUSIC

O<small>VER THE LAST QUARTER CENTURY</small>,
Baroque music has experienced a
significant rise in interest and
popularity. When speaking of the
revival of Baroque music, it is impossible not to mention Wanda
Landowska's name. For several decades she studied, discovered, and
introduced this music to wide audiences throughout the world. It
was not an easy task to change the
public perception of old and almost forgotten music. To fulfil this
mission, Landowska played concerts, lectured, published a book
and many articles, taught harpsi-
chord, and researched old manuscripts and scores.

Wanda Landowska

Landowska was born in Warsaw on July 5, 1879. Her parents were
Polish Jews converted to Catholicism. Wanda's father was a successful
lawyer, her mother was a linguist, and both of them were advanced amateur musicians. Glamorous and exciting musicales were quite often held
in Landowska's house. Among their participants were the great Italian
baritone Mattia Battistini and many distinguished Polish musicians.

Wanda started to study piano at the age of four with the well-
known pianists Aleksander Michalowski and Jan Kleczynski. Her musical passions, as well as her stubborness, were rocognized very early. She

refused to play exercises, scales and studies and did not like to study theory. But her favourite composer was J.S.Bach. When she was fourteen, the great conductor Artur Nikisch heard her playing one of the Preludes and Fugues from Bach's *The Well-Tempered Clavier*. He was so impressed with her rendition that he immediately nicknamed the young pianist "the Bacchante".

In 1896, Wanda moved to Berlin, where she studied composition with Heinrich Urban, who also taught I.Paderewski and J.Hofmann, and piano with M.Moszkowski. While in Berlin, Wanda spent long hours in the museum of the Hochschule für Musik, which housed one of the best collections of period instruments in Europe. Here she got a taste of, and fell in love with, the harpsichord.

Landowska moved to Paris in 1900 together with the musicologist Henry Lew, who became her husband. In Paris, Landowska's career as a pianist was very successful. She performed the customary nineteenth-century repertoire which was quite familiar to audiences. Gradually, however, Landowska began including pieces of Baroque composers in her programs that were either little known or unknown to Parisian audiences. Starting in 1903, she performed on both piano and harpsichord during the same concerts. Eventually she gave exclusively harpsichord recitals, an instrument which had not been heard in Paris for more than a hundred years.

In 1909, Landowska and Lew published a monograph entitled *La Musique Ancienne*.[1] In this fundamental work they flatly denied the idea of progress in musical development. They insisted that music of any period has its absolute value, and any comparison of music from different periods with regard to its relative importance does not make much sense. Both writers admitted that musical language and means of expression change with time, but they insisted that the quality and high standards of real masterpieces remain the same, regardless of the date of their composition. They came to conclusion that Baroque music is of the same importance as nineteenth-century and contemporary music and as such, should be intensively studied, popularized and performed.

Working on their book, Landowska and Lew studied hundreds of forgotten manuscripts, books, and scores of the seventeenth and eighteenth centuries from numerous libraries, archives and private collections.

While *La Musique Ancienne* was addressed to professionals, Landowska vigorously promoted Baroque music to broader audiences by publishing articles in Parisian newspapers and magazines and giving lectures and presentations. She enjoyed the support of Albert Schweitzer, who wrote about her in 1905: "Anyone who heard Wanda Landowska play the *Italian Concerto* (by J.Bach - E.Z.) on her wonderful Pleyel harpsichord finds it hard to understand how it could ever be played on a modern piano."[2]

Until 1912, Landowska played on the Pleyel instrument referred to by A. Schweitzer, but she was not fully satisfied with its quality and authenticity. At her request and under her guidance, the Pleyel company conducted extensive research and eventually designed a new version of the harpsichord. Landowska "inaugurated" this new instrument at the Bach Festival in Breslau in 1912, and it remained in her possession until her death.

Trying to revive and promote the harpsichord, Landowska went on concert tours to many countries. Her three tours in Russia in 1907, 1909 and 1913 were particularly succesful. In 1907 the distinguished Russian musicologist Professor Aleksander Ossovsky wrote about her: "She is an artist from head to foot, who is in love with the beauty of the old art. She is able to charge with this love every responsive listener. She can do this because she possesses the temperament of an exponent."[3]

In 1907, Landowska paid tribute to Leo Tolstoy, playing for him at his Yasnaya Polyana estate. On December 23rd, 1907, Tolstoy's secretary Nicolai Gusev made a note in his diary: "Landowska played on the harpsichord she brought with her. Among the pieces she played, Leo Nicolaevich liked the old French folk dances and the oriental folk songs more than others... Leaving the room, he told Landowska (in French): "Thank you not only for the pleasure provided by your music, but also for confirmation of my view on the art."[4]

Landowska also remembered her visit to Tolstoy:

> "I shall never forget the days I spent at Tolstoy's home, nor the hours I played for him. He adored music, and he knew how to listen admirably. While playing, I observed this luminous old man with his silver hair, his sweet and penetrating blue eyes, and I could see, as though reflected in a mirror, the agitation music pro-

voked in him. He drank it, was steeped in it. He purred with pleasure or burst into big, rich, and sonorous laughter. He felt each piece with such intensity that gave him a new life. Tolstoy was a creator-listener."[5]

In 1913 Hermann Kretzschmar, the director of the Berlin Hochschule für Musik, invited Landowska to establish and lead a harpsichord class there.

With the outbreak of World War I Landowska and Lew, as residents of France - an enemy country - became internees, and their rights to move and work were restricted. However, Landowska continued to teach even during the war years, both privately and at the Hochschule.

After the war, in 1918, Lew was killed in a traffic accident in Berlin, and Landowska returned to Paris, alone. On her way to France she made a stop in Basel, Switzerland, where she played the harpsichord in a performance of Bach's *St. Matthew Passion*. Since the death of the great composer in 1750, this was the first performance of the *Passion* in which a harpsichord was used in accordance with Bach's original score.

In Paris, Landowska accepted a teaching position at the *École Normale de Musique* and resumed international concert tours. She gave many harpsichord performances in the USA, Latin America, Europe and Asia. The financial success of these tours enabled her to acquire a home at Saint-Leu-la-Forêt near Paris. After significant home renovations, including construction of a small concert hall, Landowska opened her own *École de Musique Ancienne*, which attracted students from all over the world. Landowska often played harpsichord for her pupils and the audiences in the newly built hall. Here she performed all the Two-Part and Three-Part Inventions, the complete *Well-Tempered Clavier* and the *Goldberg Variations* by J. S. Bach. Her interpretation of the master was sometimes quite romantic, with a rhythmic and dynamic flexibility which could not be accepted by Bach's purists. However, Landowska's rendition of Bach was always natural and convincing.

By analogy with Bayreuth, where the specially designed theatre was built in 1878 for performing Richard Wagner's operas, Saint-Leu-la-Forêt has been dubbed "French Bayreuth."

Thanks to Landowska's energy and efforts, her school also became a research centre on Baroque music, containing more than 10,000 books and scores as well as a unique collection of period instruments.

In the 1930s, Landowska made numerous recordings in both Paris and Saint-Leu-la-Forêt. They included twnety-four Sonatas by D.Scarlatti, all Handel's Suites, the *Goldberg Variations* and the *Chromatic Fantasia and Fugue* by J. Bach.

Shortly before the German army captured Paris in 1940, Landowska was recording Sonatas by D. Scarlatti in a studio on the Avenue de la Grande Armée. Two minutes into the Sonata in G major (K490), French guns started their duel with German aircraft. Unruffled by the guns, Landowska kept playing. This original recording miraculously survived the war and was re-issued in 1994. Despite all technical efforts, the booms still can clearly be heard on EMI Classics CD remastering of Scarlatti intepretations by Landowska.

After the capitulation of France, Landowska left Saint-Leu-la-Forêt and fled to unoccupied southern France. Her house, library and collection of period instruments were looted by the Germans, and only a few of her possessions were recovered after the war. When the marionette Vichy Régime adopted anti-semitic laws, Landowska fled to Switzerland, then to Portugal and eventually to the USA. On December 7th, 1941, the sixty-two-year-old musician arrived in New York, accompanied by her pupil and long-term companion Dénise Restout and another long-term 'friend', the 1912 Pleyel harpsichord.

Despite a deep moral trauma and devastating financial losses caused by her escape from Europe, Landowska was still full of energy. Less than three months after arriving in the USA, on February 21st, 1942, she made a public appearance at the Town Hall in New York, playing the complete Bach's *Goldberg Variations*. Landoska's rendition received the highest praise from the audience and press alike. She recorded this masterpiece in 1943, and in the next six years 35,000 copies were sold. At first glance, this number seems moderate compared to one million cop ies of the same *Variations* recorded by Glenn Gould in 1981 and sold in the 1980s. However, keeping in mind that this composition was little-known in the USA at that time and that Landowska's recording was made at the peak of World War II, one should admit that 35,000 sold copies constituted a real success.

In 1947, Landowska moved from New York to Lakeville, Connecticut. There she continued both teaching and researching, with intermittent concert tours. In Lakeville, Landowska put her old idea into prac tice: in four years, from 1950 to 1954, she recorded all 48 Preludes and Fugues of Bach's *Well-Tempered Clavier.* Once a month the RCA team brought the sound-recording equipment from New York to Landowska's house in Lakeville and made a recording of one Prelude and Fugue. After two to three days in Lakeville, the team would return to the New York studio, where all necessary splicing and editing was made. When this ambitious project was completed, Landowska was 75 years old. The same year, she gave her last concert at the Frick Museum in New York.

Even once her performing career was done, she still continued to teach, make recordings and writing until the last weeks of her life. She died on August 16th, 1959.

Soon after her death, the Landowska Centre was established in her house. This unique Centre functions as a museum and a harpsichord music school. The museum contains Landowska's books, manuscripts, scores, and various other memorabilia as well as several harpsichords.

Although Landowska is well known as reviver of the harpsichord and its repertoire, she was also a brilliant pianist. It was in this capacity that she started her artistic career in the 1900s in Paris. At that time, she made her first recordings on metal cylinders. Some of them survived and were re-issued on LPs in the 1960s. In particular, Landowska's rendition of Sonata No 17 (K576) by Mozart and Sonata No 12 Op. 26 by Beethoven demonstrates her clear and precise finger technique as well as her lack of the sentimentality that was almost epidemic among pianists at the turn of the century.

Landowska continued to play many of Mozart's sonatas and concerti on the piano in the 1920s and 1930s. In her interpretation of Mozart she avoided two extremes typical of many musicians of that time: thanks to her very restricted use of the damper pedal, her tone was never extremely soft; nor, on the other hand, did she overload Mozart's texture with the heavy and rich modern piano sound. To perform Mozart in such a balanced way, Landowska carried out herself, and strongly recommended to others, the in-depth and thorough study of period instruments. She wrote:

> "...it is of prime importance for all present day pianists
> to study the resources and effects of eighteenth-cen-
> tury keyboard instruments as well as manner of ma-
> nipulating them. They should be instructed in the sci-

ence and art of creating on the modern piano a special
touch which can reproduce most faithfully the tonal
aesthetics of Mozart's time."[6]

While on concert tour in Austria before World War I, Landowska
made a special stop in Mozart's native city of Salzburg. Every day she
went to the Mozart Museum and for several hours played his music on
a piano which had been in the composer's possession. According to
Landowska, this practising made her fingers adjust to the real touch of
the eighteenth-century piano, while her ears became used to its unique
sound.

In 1931, a future well-known harpsichordist and musicologist, Ralph
Kirkpatrick, became Landowska's pupil. He was not a great fan of either her teaching approach or her interpretation of many compositions
of the Baroque period. Nevertheless, speaking on her performance of
the Sonata for two pianos by Mozart (K448) together with another
pupil, Ruggero Gerlin, Kirkpatrick stated that he "has only once heard
Mozart playing that even approached the precision, brilliance, and delicacy of hers, and the way she could turn and mold the phrases and
simply take you straight to heaven in the slow movement."[7]

One of the best Landowska's Mozart recordings is that of the *Coronation Concerto* (K537) made in Paris in 1937. After World War II it
was re-issued on LP by RCA. In this performance Landowska demonstrates an astonishing crystal-clear tone combined with beautiful sonority.

Even in the late 1940s, when Landowska devoted most of her time
to the harpsichord, the piano was not forgotten: in 1949, she played in
New York Mozart's Concerti No 13 (K415) and No 22 (K482) with
the New York Philharmonic under the baton of Leopold Stokowski.
Twenty years later, both Concerti were re-issued on LP, and this re-issue
was a great success. It represents Landowska as a pianist in her full
maturity, when she combined beauty of tone with extreme rhythmic
precision and a very natural and logical phrasing. Landowska composed
cadenzas to each of these Concerti, and her immersion in Mozart's music
was so comprehensive that it is hard to make a clear distinction between
her cadenzas and those composed by Mozart.

Landowska's sense of a style of composition, rather than the date
of its creation, dictated her choice of instrument. For example, she per
formed and recorded Mozart's late piano works such as the Rondo *alla*

Turca from Sonata No 11 (K331) and the Rondo in D major (K485) on harpsichord, while at the same time, found the piano a more suitable instrument for recording Mozart's earlier Sonatas (K283 and K333).

Among Landowska's other favourite piano composers was her compatriot, Chopin. Two cylinders with Chopin's Valses No.2 Op.62 and No.1 Op.64 played by Landowska at the beginning of the century have survived. However, despite music-lovers' expectation, she insisted that they never be re-issued.

In her last years at Lakeville, tired after lengthy harpsichord recording sessions, Landowska enjoyed playing Chopin on a piano.

Although her main subject of interest was Baroque music, she produced some interesting and highly educational writings on modern music,G as well. In 1910, she published in the Parisian *Courrier Musicale*, an article on the interpretation of Chopin's compositions. While in Russia in 1913, Landowska wrote an essay entitled *"Pourquoi la musique moderne n'est pas melodique?"* (*"Why Does Modern Music Lack Melody?"*)8 in which she vigorously defended modern composers against accusation that their compositions completely lack melodies. This essay is full of profound thoughts on the origin and character of contemporary music and is still very much worth reading.

Numerous Landowska manuscripts, articles and essays were thoroughly edited and published by D. Restout.9 For those interested in Baroque music and its performance and interpretation, this book is of great value. Many of Landowska's thoughts are quite unconventional and inspire the reader's imagination. Thus she wrote on fingering:

> "To establish a fingering, one has to reflect upon it and search. After deliberate thought and trials I finally decide to adopt one that seems to be good. I practise it a long time. It is a hard struggle; sometimes it does nottake hold. And suddenly another fingering I never thought of before comes very naturally to my fingers, and that one takes easily. That does not mean that one should leave certain phrases unfingered on the pretext that the fingers will fall into place by themselves. No. One must write down a fingering, even if it is the wrong one. Out of revolt and need for justice the true and right one may impose itself. This reminds me of my trip to

Yasnaya Polyana, Tolstoy's home. We were overtaken by a storm; terrifying snow drifts prevented the driver of the sled from recognizing where the road was. He stopped; and loosening the reins, he let the horses find the way all by themselves. I apply this same principle to certain phrases in which a planned fingering does not give satisfactory results. I wipe out the traces of that fingering, and I let the fingers find their own way. It is like an overflowing river returning to its bed."[10]

Describing the Baroque music that she admired so much, Landowska used vivid and penetrating wording:

"Ancient music! How harmful it was to name it so! Elevated upon a pompous pedestal and removed from mankind, "ancient" music has lost its own life. Why? Could it mean that it never was alive? Could we imagine Bach, whose passionate and constructive character exalts love and life in all its forms - could we imagine him composing only to show off his great knowledge of counterpoint? Did Bach, Couperin, and Scarlatti play the harpsichord to preserve historical truth, or because on this instrument they were able to express passion, joy, or despair?

No, ancient music is not "ancient"; it is young; it throbs with an exuberant and warm life which in turn gives us new life. It is thus that we must hear it. Listen to this "ancient" music, young and vibrant. Listen to it, and let yourself be carried away!"[11]

Landowska taught harpsichord for more than forty years, from 1913 to 1955. Many of her pupils became well known harpsichordists, pianists and teachers, including Clifford Curzon, Alice Ehlers, Sylvia Marlow, Edith Gerson-Kiwi, Isabel Nef, Ruggero Gerlin, Eta Harich-Schneider, Gusta Goldschmidt, Ralph Kirkpatrick, Dénise Restout and Irma Rogell. Some of them stayed with Landowska for a long time, others deserted her shortly, disliking her authoritarian and bossy style of teaching or disagreeing with her intepretation of compositions. However, everyone agreed that Landowska's lessons were uniquely effective for acquiring a solid harpsichord technique.

For developing finger technique, Landowska applied not only the old sets of exercises by Karl Tausig and Charles Hanon but also her own original exercises. She also introduced special gymnastics for finger muscles and finger coordination.

Although Landowska spent a lot of time developing and refining a pupil's technique, the main goal of her teaching remained to realize the underlying idea of each composition and the emotions associated with that idea. She told to her pupil I. Rogell:

> "They think that because this is so-called "ancient music", it is dead. But Bach was alive when he wrote this music. Couperin was alive. They lived, they suffered, they were men of wit, of emotion, of imagination. And if one does not have imagination to play this music on the harpsichord, far better to play a washboard."[12]

The Fifteen Two-Part Inventions by J.S. Bach were Landowska's Bible and she studied them with almost all her pupils. During such a study she focused her efforts on developing complete independence of the two voices and expressive phrasing for each voice. The Inventions were followed by J.S. Bach's suites, partitas and concerti; this compulsory menu followed compositions by G. Handel, J.-P. Rameau, F. Couperin, D. Scarlatti and W. Mozart.

Landowska's teaching technique and philosophy were experimental and innovative; she was always trying to introduce something new into her teaching practice. In this regard, it is of interest to read her letter of 1950 to a pupil:

> "Do not restrain me in my flight in the name of what I said a decade past during this or that lesson...Did I not share everything with all of you then, as I do today? Do you really think that I ever keep secret the best of my knowledge? But I cannot help it if, having never stopped working, I have learned a great deal, especially about this divine freedom that is to music the air without which it would die. What would you say of a scientist or of a painter who, like stagnant water, would stop his experimentation and remain still? "You will wreak havoc!" you exclaimed. Do I have to take into

consideration non-musical, clumsy people, but, worst
of all, pedants who - and this is serious - number my
thoughts, label and file them, although they understand
nothing of their spirit, anymore than they realize the
fury of my ecstasy for music?

Was music created for musicologists? Did Bach write for teachers' meetings?

The most beautiful thing in the world is, precisely, the conjunc-
tion of learning and inspiration. Oh, the passion for research and the joy
of discovery!"[13]

Landowska inspired two contemporaries, Manuel de Falla and
Francis Poulenc, to compose for harpsichord. She wrote:

> "In 1922, I spent several days in Granada with my friend
> Manuel de Falla. He was then working on his *Retablo
> de Maese Pedro*. Being on a concert tour in Spain, I
> had my harpsichord with me; and I was able to play for
> him a great deal and to tell him about the various pos-
> sibilities of the instrument. He became increasingly
> interested. On November 26th, 1922, he wrote from
> Granada, "Our conversation of yesterday, after reading
> the *Retablo* and all your precious indications on the
> use of the harpsichord, have awakened in me a multi-
> tude of ideas and projects to realize."[14]

This led de Falla to introduce the harpsichord in the orchestral score
of *El Retable*, which was premiered in 1923.

In that same year de Falla started composing his Concerto per
Clavicembalo (o Pianoforte), Flauto, Oboe, Clarinetto, Violin e Violon-
cello, dedicated to Landowska. It was completed in three years and premiered on November 5th, 1926, in Barcelona, with Landowska as one of
the soloists and de Falla conducting.

The 1923 premiere of *El Retablo* was attended by F. Poulenc, who
remembered:

> "It was there that I met Wanda Landowska, who was
> playing the harpsichord in Falla's *Retablo*. It was the
> first time that the harpsichord had entered a modern
> orchestra. I was fascinated by the work and by Wanda.

"Write a concerto for me", she said. I promised her to
try. My encounter with Landowska was a capital event
in my career. I have for her as much artistic respect as
human tenderness. I am proud of her friendship, and I
shall never be able to say how much I owe her."[15]

Later Poulenc described his work on this concerto:

"I wrote the *Concert Champêtre* from October 1927
to September 1928, or rather I wrote it for the first
time. You know that Wanda Landowska is an interpreter of genius... I worked with her on the first version of my concerto. We went over it note by note,
measure by measure. We did not, however, change a
measure or a melodic line, but the keyboard writing
and the choice of the instruments for the orchestra were
the chief aims of our most extensive research. Above
all, we clarified the writing, either by condensing chords
or by suppressing notes, since the multiplication of
notes is accomplished by the harpsichord itself by
means of its registers. In short, we achieved a score
whose appearance of simplicity will probably surprise
you, whose effect remains, however, rich and varied."[16]

The *Concert Champêtre ("Pastoral Concerto")* was premiered in
Paris on May 3rd, 1929, with Landowska as a soloist and Pierre Monteux
conducting the Orchestre Symphonique de Paris. This composition remained in Landowska's repertoire for many years. In November, 1949,
she performed it in New York with the New York Philharmonic under
the baton of Stokovski. A tape of this performance was sent to the
composer, who responded:

"How can I tell you my emotion at hearing my god-
dess play the *Champêtre?* What joy you gave me! I suddenly felt rejuvenated, happy... Now that I wonder
every day if my music will live, you have given me the
illusion that it will. For this, thank you from the bot-
tom of my heart."[17]

Landowska herself composed numerous works, including a *Hebrew
Poem* for orchestra, a *Liberation Fanfare* for band, Variations for two
pianos, and some other keyboard pieces and songs. She also made tran-

scriptions of contredances by Mozart and waltzes by Schubert and Joseph Lanner. Among her keyboard compositions, the most important are cadenzas for concertos by Handel, Haydn, and Mozart which are still performed by pianists and harpsichordists today. Unfortunately, many of her manuscripts were lost during World War II and have never been recovered.

Landowska possessed a unique combination of talents infrequent in the twentieth century - she was a teacher, researcher, composer and performer. Her versatile activities made her a leading figure in reviving and disseminating Baroque music and preserving the continuity of music development.

Notes

1. Landowska, W. et Lew, H., *La Musique Ancienne*, Paris, 1909.

2. Sachs, Harvey, *Virtuoso*, Thames and Hudson, London,1982, p. 158.

3. Maikapar, Aleksander, *Slovo o Vande Landowskoy (A Word on Wanda Landowska)*, In: *Vanda Landowskaya o muzike (Vanda Landowska on Music)*, Moscow, Raduga, 1991, p. 398.

4. Ibid., pp. 398-399.

5. *Landowska on Music*, Collected, edited and translated by Denise Restout, assisted by Robert Hawkins. Stein and Day, New York, 1965, p. 353 (hereafter *Landowska on Music*).

6. Ibid., p. 307.

7. Kirkpatrick, Ralph, "European Journal". *High Fidelity/ Musical America* 35, November 1985: 33-37.

8. *Landowska on Music*, op. cit., pp. 336-340.

9. See note 5.

10. *Landowska on Music*, op. cit., pp. 373-374.

11. Ibid., p. 408.

12. Rogel, Irma, "Memories of Landowska". *Clavier* 19, n. 2, 1980: 29-30.

13. *Landowska on Music*, op. cit., pp. 365-366.

14. Ibid., p. 346.

15. Poulenc, Francis, *Entretiens avec Claude Rostand (Conversations with Claude Rostand)*, Paris, Rene Julliard, 1954, 225p.

16. Poulenc, Francis, interview with Lucien Chevallier, in 1929. In: Palmer, Larry, "The Concertos of Falla and Poulenc," *The Diapason*, 70, July 1979: 9-11.

17. From the notes to the PL recording, written by Dénise Restout. in Palmer, Larry, "The Concertos of Falla and Poulenc," *The Diapason* 70, July 1979: 9-11.

SAMUEL SAMOSUD

PIONEER OF MODERN
RUSSIAN OPERA

THE TWENTIETH CENTURY HAS demonstrated a continuous movement towards specialization. The field of conducting is no exception. Many conductors of this century have concentrated their efforts on the pure symphonic genre, some have realized their talents in ballet productions, while others have opted to reign in the world's opera houses. Among those in the last group, the great Russian conductor Samuel Samosud should not be forgotten.

Samuel Samosud

Samosud was born in Tiflis, Georgia, on 14 May, 1884. His father was a conductor at the local opera company. Samuel studied wind instruments and cello, first with his father, later at the Tiflis Music College, from which he graduated in 1905. The following year, the young musician went to Prague, where he studied cello with Hans Whihan and conducting with Karel Kovarovic, a conductor and the director of the National Theatre. Samosud completed his musical education at the Schola Cantorum in Paris, where he studied with Vincent d'Indy and Edouard Colonne. While in Paris he also studied cello with Pablo Casals.

In 1910, Samosud returned to Russia and settled in St. Petersburg. His musical career began as a cellist in the People's House Opera

Theatre. It was not long, however, before he assumed the post of conductor. In the first few years he performed such operas as *Faust, Lakme, Carmen,* and Eduard Naprávnik's *Dubrovsky.*

During the 1916 season, Samosud conducted Aleksander Dargomyzhsky's *Rusalka.* The success of this production was virtually guaranteed by the presence of the Russian bass Feodor Chaliapin, who sang the role of the Millman. Chaliapin was a most demanding musician, who expected his conductors to produce performances that were in total compliance with his musical and dramatic interpretation of the characters he performed. His high artistic standards, which were often enforced by an eruptive temper, caused numerous conflicts between Chaliapin and several leading operatic conductors of the day. Surprisingly, from the first rehearsal of *Rusalka,* the relationship between the world-renowned bass and the young Samosud was very cooperative and virtually trouble-free. Many years later Samosud remembered:

> "Mark Golynkin,[1] who usually conducted all operas in which Chaliapin sang, was ill; I was asked to replace him. Due to my young age, Chaliapin approved this replacement, but only with serious reservations. After the first performance of *Rusalka,* I conducted almost all the operas that Chaliapin sang at the People's House Theatre. Daily contacts and discussions with him revealed to me that the art of the opera could indeed be elevated to new levels of excellence."[2]

Another star of the Russian opera scene was Nicolai Pechkovsky,[3] the most celebrated interpreter of the character Hermann in Tchaikovsky's *Queen of Spades.* He, too, began his career at the People's House Opera Theatre under Samosud's direction.

In 1918, Maestro Samosud accepted the position of music director at the newly established Maly Opera Theatre (Malegot), a post which he held for the next eighteen years. It was his tenure at Malegot that provided him the opportunity to rise from relative obscurity to become a prominent and influential figure in the Soviet operatic world. Samosud was an authoritarian conductor, who kept all elements of an opera's productions under his strict, personal supervision. Beyond his attention to all details of production, he tried to achieve the highest standard in every facet of the *mise-en-scène* and made no distinction between the major and minor components of an operatic performance. To him, a performer's hairstyle or choreographic movements were equally important as singing with accurate pitch. All his efforts as a conductor were focused on delivering the composer's intentions and musical ideas with the maximum level of clarity and expressiveness.

The composer Ivan Dzerzhinsky,[4] whose opera *Tihiy Don (Quiet Flows the Don)* was premiered by Samosud at the Malegot in 1935, said of the conductor:

> "He knows the opera theatre as does nobody else. He is highly respected by everybody for his refined culture, his great courage, his hard work, and his ability to convince other performers to work hard. To him, everything is important as far as opera production is concerned. You can see him talking with the set and costume designers as well as with the stagehands. During the rehearsal he often leaves the conductor's podium to work with the stage director on the *mise-en-scène*, to show a striking gesture to a singer, to explain a complicated segment of a score to the chorus, or to give advice on the set design. Samosud is an opera director in the true sense of the word, who shapes his productions in accordance with a detailed and thorough plan. As a result, his directions to performers are always clear and confident."[5]

Under Samosaud's strong leadership, Malegot was one of the best opera companies in the USSR and became a successful rival to such renowned and respected theatres as the Moscow's Bolshoi and Leningrad's Kirov. There was, however, a significant difference between them. While the old opera theatres emphasized the mainstream repertoire of Mozart, Rossini, Puccini, Verdi, Bizet, Tchaikovsky, and Mussorgsky, Samosud made extraordinary efforts to enlarge this repertoire to include new operas of Western and Soviet composers. At Malegot he gave the Russian premieres of such modern operas as *Jonny Spielt auf* by Ernst Krenek and *Der arme Columbus* by Erwin Dressel.

When working with young and often inexperienced operatic composers, Samosud was always ready to give efficient assistance to improve the orchestration, vocal parts, and even librettos of their compositions. Under Samosud's baton, many operas of such Soviet composers as Ivan

Dzerzhinsky, Valery Zhelobinsky,[6] Victor Voloshinov,[7] Arseny Gladkovsky,[8] and others were premiered on the Malegot stage during the 1920s and 1930s. At this time, the theatre was praised as "a laboratory of the Soviet opera" by critics and opera lovers.

Understandably, not all new operas became part of the Malegot's permanent repertoire, but some, such as *Nos (The Nose)* and *Ledi Macbet Mtsenskogo Uyezda (The Lady Macbeth of the Mtsensk District)* by Dmitri Shostakovich, became landmark achievements in Soviet operatic history.

The Nose was completed in the summer of 1928. Its libretto was based on several stories by Nicolai Gogol and a small segment of Feodor Dostoyevsky's *The Brothers Karamazov.* It is an avant-garde masterpiece in which Shostakovich experimented with and discovered new possibilities in opera. The opera's vocal segments can better be described as recitatives than traditional arias. Although Shostakovich's recitatives follow the traditions of Aleksander Dargomyzhsky's and Modest Mussorgsky's musical realism, they are innovative. According to the composer's remarks, recitatives of the leading character, the Nose, should be performed by a singer clutching his nose. Major Kovalyov's vocal part contains prolonged vocalising of consonants. Matching the unconventional effects of the vocal writing were those in the orchestration. Here, Shostakovich depicted a horse's stomp, a drunken man's hiccup, and even Major Kovalyov's shaving. The operatic score is thus saturated with extreme vocal and instrumental difficulties. During *The Nose's* lengthy rehearsal period, Samosud achieved a perfect balance of ensemble, and the singers demonstrated an almost unheard-of virtuosity during the performances of their complicated recitatives.

The work's première occurred on January 18th, 1930. It received a mixed critical response. Among the opera's strong supporters were the writer Yury Tynjanov, film directors Gregory Kozintsev and Leonid Trauberg, musicologists Boris Asafiev[9] and IvanSollertinsky,[10] and the pianist Leonid Nikolaev.[11] For the most part, those who harshly criticized *The Nose* were either members of the leftist Russian Association of Proletarian Music, or Soviet musical bureaucrats. Both groups accused Shostakovich of "formalism" and "being out of touch with real life". This ideologically-motivated criticism was so severe that after sixteen performances, the opera was withdrawn from the

Malegot repertoire. After the Second World War, *The Nose* was staged by several European opera companies, but not until 1974 was it revived in Russia by Gennady Rozhdestvensky on the stage of the Moscow Chamber Opera Theatre.

While *The Nose* was full of parody and the grotesque, the second Shostakovich opera, *The Lady Macbeth of the Mtsensk District*, portrays genuine characters and intense emotions. This opera was completed in December 1932. The complexity of its orchestral accompaniment and vocal parts required an extended rehearsal period. Samosud rehearsed *Lady Macbeth* in close collaboration with the composer for almost a year. The premiére occurred on 22 January, 1934, and was received with enthusiasm. Shostakovich was delighted with the production and praised Samosud for its success. Subsequently, when Shostakovich wanted to convey approval of a performance of one of his operas, he usually said: "This conductor reminds me of Samosud," a compliment which connoted the composer's highest approbation[12].

In 1934 and 1935, *Lady Macbeth* was staged with great success by several Russian, European, and American opera companies. It seemed that this masterpiece would remain in the Russian opera theatre's repertoire for many years to come. However, the new opera became a focal point of a political campaign skillfully orchestrated by Stalin. On 18 January, 1936, a destructive editorial entitled "Muddle Instead of Music" appeared in the Communist Party newspaper *Pravda*. There were rumours that it was written by Stalin himself; but it is more likely that the writer was the party spokesman, journalist David Zaslavsky. Sharing the role of villain with Shostakovich were many other intellectuals who either did not follow Communist Party directives or resisted orthodox Communist ideology. *Pravda's* language was harsh and aggressive: "Starting from the first minute, the audience is stunned and shocked by a deliberately discordant and chaotic stream of sounds. Shreds of melodies, embryos of musical phrases sink and disappear in the rumble, gnash and scream. It is impossible to follow this 'music'; no one can remember it."[13]

It is not surprising that, the day after this editorial was published, the opera was banned and withdrawn from the repertoires of all Soviet opera theatres. Its revised version, *Katerina Izmaylova*, reappeared on the Soviet operatic scene in the early 1960s, and since then, this version of Shostakovich's masterpiece has been performed with increasing success by many Russian opera companies.

In 1936, Samosud was appointed the music director of the Bolshoi Theatre in Moscow, the largest and most famous Soviet opera theatre, which also was the recipient of Stalin's personal patronage. Although this position was highly answerable to the Communist Party bureaucrats and ideologists and vulnerable to all sorts of criticism, the conductor continued his renewal of the operatic repertoire. Under Samosud's direction, revised versions of two great Russian operas by Mikhail Glinka, *Ivan Susanin* (formerly *A Life for the Tsar*) and *Ruslan and Ludmila*, were staged. Samosud also continued working in close collaboration with young Soviet opera composers, thereby having a significant influence on many new opera productions. Under his baton such operas as *Podnyataya Tselina (Virgin Soil Upturned)* by Ivan Dzerzhinsky and *V Ogne (Into the Fire)* by Dmitri Kabalevsky were premiered at the Bolshoi Theatre. Samosud's ongoing commitment to innovative repertoire caused significant tension between him and high-ranking Soviet musical bureaucrats. Finally, in 1943, he was fired from the Bolshoi.

During the war years, collaboration between Samosud and Shostakovich extended beyond the operatic field. On 5 March, 1942, in the city of Kuibyshev, the conductor led the world première of Shostakovich's Seventh Symphony, the *Leningrad*, which was broadcast throughout the USSR. The Moscow première occurred on 29 March, 1942, under Samosud's baton and was broadcast not only in Russia but also abroad.

Forced to leave the Bolshoi Theatre, Samosud joined the Stanislavsky-Nemirovich-Danchenko Music Theatre in Moscow. Singers who performed at the theatre during that time such as Nadezhda Kemarskaya, Tatyana Yanko, and Sergei Tsenin, recalled :

> "Samosud's rehearsals were unforgettable. Whether he was rehearsing the merry operetta *Der Bettelstudent* by Karl Millöcker, or the dramatic opera *Lubov' Yarovaya* by Vladimir Enke,[14] or the comic opera *Frol Skobeev*
>
> by Tikhon Khrennikov, he was able to explain the most essential features of each character. Following his guidance, each singer went through the experience and joy associated with the role to be performed."[15]

Samosud was closely associated with the rehearsal and production of one of the best Soviet operas, *Voyna i mir (War and Peace)* by Sergei Prokofiev. The conductor heard the first version of the score in May 1942, performed in a piano four-hand reduction by Sviatoslav Richter and Anatoly Vedernikov. Despite its being incomplete, Samosud was so impressed with its grandeur and innovation that he instantly decided to stage it.

In 1942 and 1943, Sasmosud worked tirelessly with Prokofiev to make this epic opera suitable for performance at the Bolshoi Theatre. Although this productive collaboration was abruptly terminated when Samosud was fired from the Bolshoi, he remained preoccupied with the idea of a *War and Peace* production.

In 1945, Samosud was invited to resume his position as guest music director of Malegot in Leningrad. He agreed to take the post with the condition that the theatre would stage *War and Peace*. The conductor's stipulation was accepted, and vast government funds were committed to allow rehearsals to begin. As usual, Samosud's efforts were not limited to conducting; his close collaboration with Prokofiev shaped the musical form of the new production. The conductor recalled:

> In the scene "The Council in Fili", Kutuzov's aria held great importance. I remember at least eight versions, apart from many minor changes and clarifications. The earlier versions were interesting enough, but they lacked something important and essential. In my view this aria should express the main patriotic theme of the opera, as well as the historical importance of the depicted event. It should also portray Kutuzov as a human being, the peculiarity of his character and intellect; and above all, it should be an aria in the true sense of the word; it should be a piece of vocal music.

> "What do you eventually want?" Prokofiev asked me nervously, after my rejection of yet another version. "I want any aria to be the focal point of the scene, like those in *Ivan Susanin* or *Prince Igor*," I told him. "I cannot do this," Prokofiev replied.

> "I know that you can do better. You cannot *but* do it," I insisted.

The next day Prokofiev brought the next version, and I had to say again: "This is not what I want." He asked: "Do you want to say that it is not to your taste, or does not suit you?" I agreed: "It is not to my taste, but could you imagine what will happen if we express a view contradicting our taste?"

One day, when we had lost all hope, he gave me a piece of paper with a melody written on it. It was a background song of the Russian warriors from the composer's early score to Sergei Eisenstein's film, *Ivan the Terrible*. Triumphantly he told me: "It seems to me that this is exactly what you want."

To say that I wanted it was the same as to say nothing. It was the melody I had dreamt of, very Russian, heart-penetrating, with a long breath. It gave a perfect musical image of the Motherland and the victory. At the same time, this melody fully depicted Kutuzov's character and personality. The Kutuzov aria has become one of the most expressive and powerful of the opera's leitmotifs.[16]

The first part of the opera, consisting of eight scenes, was first performed in concert in Moscow on 7 June, 1945, and at Malegot on 12 June, 1946, both times under Samosud's baton. After these successful productions, Prokofiev wrote: "The conductor's extensive knowledge of the opera score and our long collaboration during preparation of the opera's concert perfomancein Moscow have enabled Samosud to penetrate deeply into my artistic conception."[17] The Leningrad première was also a tremendous success, and by March 1947, fifty sold-out performances had been given. In the summer of that year, Samosud conducted the dress rehearsal of the opera's second part; once again, however, a political storm washed away the long-awaited première. On 10 February, 1948, the Communist Party Central Committee published a decree on the opera *Velikaya Druzhba (The Great Friendship)* by Vano Muradeli, which condemned leading Soviet composers, including Prokofiev and Shostakovich, as formalists and decadents. Following this decree, both parts of *War and Peace* were banned and withdrawn from the repertoire.

Although deeply disappointed by this development, Samosud never ceased his efforts to move the opera forward to a public performance. Due to his devotion and energy, nine of its scenes were broadcast on USSR radio in 1953. Only after Stalin's death was Samosud able to prepare thirteen scenes for a one-evening performance at the Stanislavsky-Nemirovich-Danchenko Music Theatre. Unfortunately, a few days before this première, Samosud became seriously ill, and the first performance, on 8 November, 1957, was conducted by his assistant, Aleksander Shaverdov. Following the performance, Samosud wrote: "I fulfilled my promise given to Prokofiev at the time he started to work on *War and Peace*. His ingenious opera has at last been performed in its entirety and included in the opera theatre's repertoire. This is true happiness!"[17]

Prokofiev expressed his appreciation of Samosud's conducting by asking him to première many of his post-war symphonic and choral compositions. These included *The Ode to the End of the War* (1945), the cantata *The Winter Bonfire* (1950), the oratorio *On Guard for Peace* (1950), the *Wedding Suite* and the *Gypsy Fantasy* from the ballet *The Stone Flower* (1951), *Pushkin Waltzes* (1952), *A Festive Poem - the Meeting of the Volga and the Don* (1952), and the Seventh Symphony.

During the years preceding his death in 1964, Samosud was a principal conductor of the Moscow Philharmonic. Although this post led him to perform mostly symphonic repertoire, he was able to remain involved with his life-long love, opera. Under his direction *Lohengrin* and *Die Meistersinger von Nürnberg* by Wagner, *L'Italiana in Algeri* and *La Gazza Ladra* by Rossini, and *Charodeyka (The Sorceress)* by Tchaikovsky were performed in concert.

Samosud exerted a major influence on the development of modern Russian opera. His productions of *The Nose, The Lady Macbeth of the Mtsensk District,* and *War and Peace* are still considered pinnacles of Russian opera.

Notes

1. Golynkin, Mark, (1875-1963), conductor at the People's House Opera Theatre in St. Petersburg (1912), guest conductor at the Mariinsky theatre (1918), emigrated to Palestine (1923), became music director of the Israeli Opera Theatre (1948).

2. *Sovremennye dirizhery (Contemporary Conductors)*, Sovetskiy Kompozitor, Moscow, 1969, p. 228

3. Pechkovsky, Nicolai, (1896-1966), renowned Russian dramatic tenor, soloist at the Kirov (formerly Mariinsky) Theatre (1924-1941). His performance of the role of Hermann in Tchaikovsky's *Queen of Spades* was admired by audiences and highly regarded by critics. During the Second World War he stayed within German-occupied territories and sang in Prague and Vienna. He was imprisoned for treason in 1944 and released in 1954. Although he never returned to the operatic stage, he concertized and taught extensively in Russia in the 1950s and 1960s.

4. Dzerzhinsky, Ivan, (1909-1978), composer. His opera *Tihiy Don (Quiet Flows the Don)* was considered by the Soviet authorities as a model of a socialist-realism opera and quite the opposite of those written by Shostakovich. Compositions: eight operas, including *Tihiy Don (Quiet Flows the Don, 1934)*, *Podnyataya Tselina (Virgin Soil Upturned, 1937)*, *Grigori Melehov (Gregory Melekhov, 1967)*; two tone poems; three piano concerti; and others.

5. *Sovremennye*, op. cit., p. 229.

6. Valery Zhelobinsky (1913-1946), composer, pianist, teacher at the Tambov Music College (1942). Compositions: three operas; two operettas; three piano concerti; and others.

7. Voloshinov, Victor, (1905-1960), composer and teacher, professor at the Leningrad Conservatory (1955). Compositions: two operas; concerto for violin and organ; songs; and others.

8.   Gladkovsky, Arseny, (1894-1945), composer, graduated from the Leningrad Conservatory (1924). Compositions: an opera; a ballet; three symphonies; chamber and incidental music.

9.   Asafiev, Boris, (1884-1949) (literary pseudonym Igor Glebov), musicologist, composer, and critic, professor at the Leningrad Conservatory (1925), head of the Soviet Composers' Union (1948). He supported *The Nose* but withdrew his support for *Lady Macbeth*. He severely criticized Prokofiev and Shostakovich during the 1948 campaign. Compositions: ten operas; twenty seven ballets; three symphonies; and others. Books: *Selected Works* in five volumes, Moscow, 1952.

10. Sollertinsky, Ivan, (1902-1944), musicologist, artistic director of the Leningrad Philharmonic (1927), professor at the Leningrad Conservatory (1939), brilliant music reviewer and lecturer. From 1927 he was a close friend of Shostakovich.

11. Nikolaev, Leonid, (1878-1942), pianist, composer, and remarkable piano teacher, professor at the Leningrad Conservatory. Among his pupils were Shostakovich, Yudina, and Sofronitsky.

12. *Pis'ma k drugu: Dmitri Shostakovich - Isaaku Glikmanu. (Letters to a Friend: Dmitri Shostakovich to Isaak Glikman).* Sovetskiy Kompozitor-"DSCH", Moscow-St. Petersburg, 1993, p. 37.

13. *Pravda*, 18 January, 1936.

14. Enke, Vladimir, (1908-1987), composer, critic, and theorist, graduated from the Moscow Conservatory (1936). Compositions: two operas; two operettas; a symphony; three piano sonatas; and others.

15. *Sovremennye*, op. cit., p. 230.

16. *Prokofiev, Sergei , 1953-1963, Stat'i i materialy. (Sergei Prokofiev 1953-1963. Articles and Materials* Compiled by Israel Nest'ev and Grigori Edel'man*). . Sovetskiy Kompozitor, Moscow, 1962, pp. 141-143.

17. Ibid., p. 109.

18. Ibid., p. 158

Table of Selected Premieres and Revivals
Conducted by Samuel Samosud

Composer	Work	Ensemble	Date
Shostakovich	*The Nose*	Malegot	18.01.30
Gladkovsky	*The Front and the Rear*	Malegot	07.11.30
Zhelobinsky	*The Kamarino Peasant*	Malegot	
Shostakovich	*The Lady McBeth of the Mtsenk District*	Malegot	22.01.31
Zhelobinsky	*The Name-Day*	Malegot	26.03.35
Dzerzhinsky	*Quiet Flows the Don*	Malegot	22.10.35
Glinka	*Ruslan and Ludmila*	Bolshoi Theater	14.04.37
Dzerzhinky	*Virgin Soil Upturned*	Bolshoi Theater	23.10.37
Glinka	*Ivan Susanin*	Bolshoi Theater	21.02.39
Tchaikovsky	*Yolanta*	Bolshoi Theater	19.10.40
Shostakovich	*Symphony N.7 Leningrad*	Kuibyshev Symphony	05.03.42
Tchaikovsky	*Queen of Spades*	Bolshoi Theater	20.10.42
Prokofiev	*War and Peace (the first part, 8 scenes)*	Malegot	12.06.46
Kabalevsky	*The Taras Family*	Stanislavsky-Nemirovich Danchenko Music Theater	02.11.47
Khrennikov	*Frol Skobeev*	Stanislavsky-Nemirovich Danchenko Music Theater	24.02.50
Prokofiev	*The Strone Flower Gypsy Fantasy*	Moscow Philharmonic	18.11.51
Prokofiev	*The Stone Flower*	Moscow Philharmonic	12.12.51
Prokofiev	*Symphony N.7*	Moscow Philharmonic	11.10.52

6

A GREAT MUSICAL SAGA

THREE GENERATIONS OF THE NEUHAUS FAMILY

IN THE HISTORY OF MUSIC, THERE are several examples of outstanding talent transmitted through several generations in the same family. Probably the best example of this is J.S. Bach and his sons. In modern times, the phenomenon can be best exemplified by the Neuhaus family.

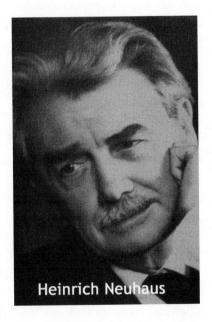

Heinrich Neuhaus

The founder of this musical dynasty, Gustav Neuhaus (1847-1937), was born in Kalkar, Germany, where his father owned a handicraft piano factory. Gustav studied piano at the Cologne Conservatory with the distinguished professor Ernst Rudorff, who later taught Leopold Godovsky. In 1874, Neuhaus left Germany and went to Russia. He settled in Elizavetgrad in Ukraine and established a private music school. This school was well known for its high teaching standards and was well-regarded not only by the local musical community and residents but also by Rimsky-Korsakov and Glazunov. Among Neuhaus' students were two of his relatives, the great Polish composer Karol Szymanowski and the famous Russian pianist, conductor, composer and teacher Felix Blumenfeld,[1] who later taught Simon Barere, Vladimir Horowitz and Maria Grinberg.

Gustav expressed keen interest not only in teaching but also in various aspects of the art of the piano. In 1906, he published a brochure entitled *Das Natürliche Notensystem (The Natural System of Notation)*, in which he proposed a new system of notation based on the disposition of white and black keys on the keyboard. Later he invented the slightly curved keyboard, which provided an equal distance from the player to each key.

Gustav's wife, Olga Neuhaus (née Blumenfeld, 1859-1937), was a sister of Felix Blumenfeld and, like all members of their family, was very musically-gifted. She started to teach piano at the age of fourteen and, after marriage, helped Gustav to establish and run the family's music school. Their daughter Natalie was born in 1884 and their son Heinrich four years later.

The children were plunged into music from birth. Their parents' school was located in their house and every day they heard students of various levels playing piano. Quite often their parents performed piano duos, and brother and sister were the most devoted listeners. At the age of six both children started piano lessons - first with their mother and afterwards with their father.

In 1902 the Neuhaus family travelled through Germany. At that time, Heinrich already had an extensive repertoire, consisting of compositions by Beethoven, Chopin, Schumann and Liszt. Next year, the younger Neuhaus made a successful début in Düsseldorf, after which the family returned to Elizavetgrad.

Following Blumenfeld's advice, Heinrich and Natalie went to Berlin in 1905 to study with Leopold Godowsky. For almost two years following, Heinrich had one lesson per month with one of the best pianists of the post-Rubinstein era. As early as the third lesson, they argued about Chopin's Concerto in E minor. Despite Godowsky's beauty of touch and delicate phrasing, Neuhaus found his teacher's performance slightly mannered and proposed his own interpretation of this popular composition. After this confrontation, Godowsky often told Neuhaus with a slight laugh: "You have your own individuality, and I am not going to oppress it."[2] Much later, in May of 1935, when Godowsky was performing in Moscow, he presented his picture to Heinrich with the following dedication: "To a genuine man, genius and noble artist from a devoted friend."

At the age of sixteen, Neuhaus made two public appearances in Berlin, playing the Concerto in F minor by Chopin. Both performances were great successes and received many favourable reviews in Berlin's newspapers.

For medical reasons, the young musician went to Italy in 1906 and stayed in Florence for almost a year. According to his memoirs, it was the happiest year in his life. Neuhaus liked the picturesque Italian landscapes, the Italian arts and Italians themselves. He studied Italian, visited museums and played the piano with new inspiration.

In 1912, Heinrich resumed lessons with Godowsky, who was then teaching at the Academy of Music in Vienna. After two years, he graduated from the Academy with a special award and returned to Elizavetgrad in 1914, shortly before the outbreak of the First World War.

While in Vienna, Neuhaus received several invitations to make concert tours in Europe and North America, but they were all cancelled due to the war.

In 1918 Neuhaus moved to Kiev, where he was appointed a professor in the Kiev Conservatory. He taught piano for almost fifty years, first in Kiev and then in Moscow.

In Kiev, Neuhaus continued to pursue his concert career. Despite the tremendous hardship caused by the Civil War in Ukraine, musical life in Kiev was thriving. The piano duo of Neuhaus and Blumenfeld played transcriptions of Wagner's operas and Scriabin's symphonies in the freezing Conservatory concert hall. Another piano duo, Neuhaus and Horowitz, presented breathtaking performances and amazed the Kiev audience. Together with the refined violinist Paul Kohansky, Neuhaus gave a series of concerts in which they performed all the Beethoven Sonatas for violin and piano. Very often Neuhaus appeared on the Kiev concert stage as a soloist, playing Chopin, Schumann, Brahms and Scriabin. He was the first pianist to perform all ten piano Sonatas by Scriabin in Kiev, and these performances of relatively new and unknown compositions became a musical extravaganza in the city's cultural life. The compulsiveness, delicacy, ecstatic mood and sensuality of Scriabin's music matched Neuhaus' own artistic temperament. At the same time, he continued to teach intensively at the Kiev Conservatory.

One of his students, Theodore Gutman, who later became a professor at the Gnessin Institute in Moscow, wrote:

> Unusual musical impressions forced me to stay in the Neuhaus' studio for hours. Every day he discovered a new vision of well known compositions. He captivated us entirely with his unconventional playing, singing and conducting. Nothing recalled the trivial lesson when the student plays and the teacher makes comments and corrections. Discussing our performances, Neuhaus gave us vivid comparisons and numerous examples of various musical styles and interpretations. It created a very artistic and wonderful environment in this studio.[3]

Among his students in the Kiev Conservatory were Nathan Perelman and Vera Razumowska, both of whom later became famous professors at the Leningrad Conservatory.

In 1922, Neuhaus moved to Moscow to become a full-time professor at the Moscow Conservatory. He was equally active as a teacher and a concert pianist. The following year, to mark his arrival in the capital, Neuhaus repeated performances of ten Scriabin Sonatas. The reviewer of the Moscow newspaper *Zrelisha (Entertainment)* wrote about these concerts:

> You could argue about Neuhaus' interpretation of some of Sonatas, but there is no doubt that he possesses a very personal style and expressiveness. The pianist demonstrates an in-depth interpretation of Scriabin's musical ideas and inspires listeners with realization of this music. Nobody can remain indifferent at these concerts, and there is a general agreement that Neuhaus' performance is highly artistic and very convincing.[4]

In the 1920s and 1930s, Neuhaus played not only conventional classical repertoire but also the contemporary music of Aleksandrov, Miaskovsky, Feinberg, Kreyn[5] and his cousin Szymanowski.

Neuhaus' fame as a teacher grew. Each of his lessons was, in fact, a master class, which was given not only for his own students but for all "strangers" interested in the art of piano- playing. Often, after finish ing lessons in the Conservatory, he invited young musicians to his very modest and tiny apartment, where they continued playing music and openly discussed compositions, their interpretations and various performing styles. Such informal contacts extended the musical horizon of his students enormously. Neuhaus was fluent in Polish, German, French, Italian and Latin and was very well acquainted with European literature, philosophy, and art. During piano lessons he inspired students' imagination by giving them examples and analogies from all these fields.

Neuhaus was a poetry-lover and knew by heart many verses of Virgil and Horace, Roncard and Verlaine, Pushkin and Pasternak, who was his close friend and an admirer. Neuhaus liked to quote various poets in order to awaken the creative imagination of his students – challenging monotonous, bleak and routine playing.

Neuhaus' knowledge of musical literature was astonishing. In the course of a lesson he could play by heart long segments from operas, symphonies, trios, quartets and countless piano compositions.

Before the Second World War, Neuhaus worked with hundreds of students. According to his own recollection, he dealt with "students of all levels of talent, from almost defective to genius, with the whole spectrum of gifts in between." In 1935, nineteen-year-old Emil Gilels was admitted to the Moscow Conservatory and became Neuhaus' student. Two years later Sviatoslav Richter started to study with Neuhaus. Richter kept up an admiring and very close personal and artistic relationship with his teacher until Neuhaus' death. In 1937, Neuhaus' postgraduate student Yakov Zak won the first prize at the Chopin International Competition in Warsaw.

Soon after the outbreak of the war between Russia and Germany, in November of 1941, Heinrich Neuhaus was arrested by the KGB. The accusation laid against him seems laughable now, but was extremely dangerous in the "Stalinist" Russia during the war - specifically, as a Russian German, he was accused of not having left Moscow, waiting for the capital's capture by the advancing German army. For eight months he was imprisoned in the KGB's Lubyanka jail in Moscow, where he was interrogated and beaten. However, even in these extreme conditions, he maintained his strong sense of humour. Soon after the war was over, talking with his daughter-in-law, he remembered: "Do you know when I was most proud of myself? During my last interrogation in Lubyanka the KGB officer who conducted the investigation ordered his assistant: 'Bring me the second volume of the Neuhaus' case!' At that moment I thought I must be a very important person, if two complete volumes had been written about me."[6]

Thanks to the intervention of Gilels, Heinrich's imprisonment ended in August of 1942, when he was exiled from Moscow to Sverdlovsk (Ekaterinburg) with all his Moscow property and belongings confiscated. In September, he started work in the Sverdlovsk Conservatory, and without lodging, slept in the same studio where he taught. During the daytime, the small studio could not accommodate all the students and teachers who wanted to attend Neuhaus' lessons. Shortly after his arrival in Sverdlovsk he started public performances. During the winter, he played in unheated concert halls, wearing a winter cotton jacket and gloves with cut-off fingers.

Neuhaus returned to Moscow in 1944 and resumed his professorial duty at the Moscow Conservatory. Students and teachers from many Soviet cities and later from other parts of Europe came to his studio #29, in order to be taught, inspired and mesmerized by his artistic spirit. His students won countless piano competitions both in the USSR and abroad. He prepared not only brilliant soloists but also many famous teachers who still work in many Russian and European Conservatories. Neuhaus did not limit his teaching to the Moscow Conservatory. Every year, he travelled through the USSR, giving master classes and lectures in Leningrad, Kiev, Tbilisi, Yerevan, Riga, Tallinn and many other cities. Despite his enormous work load at the Moscow Conservatory and his gradually deteriorating health, Neuhaus continued concert tours, giving in some seasons from 30 to 40 performances.

In 1958, Neuheus published a book entitled *The Art of Piano Playing*,[7] in which he described his ideas and thoughts on piano-playing, teaching and the interpretation of various piano compositions. It is a summary of his unique teaching and performing experience and a textbook to all interested in the art of the piano. Within a few years it was translated into almost thirty languages.

Owing to serious health problems Neuhaus ceased public performances by the end of the 1950s but still continued to work intensively with graduates and postgraduates in the Moscow Conservatory. He died of heart failure on the 10th of November, 1964.

Heinrich Neuhaus was one of the last representatives of the Romantic tradition of pianists. His performances were always inspiring, poetic and had an improvised quality. At the same time, he was a thinker and explorer. In his performances, he was able to combine vivid expression with deep knowledge and understanding of a composer's conception and musical forms.Neuhaus remains one of the greatest interpreters of Scriabin and Chopin, music which perfectly corresponded to his artistic temperament and taste.

Neuhaus was one of the greatest piano teachers of the twentieth century, dubbed by contemporaries "Heinrich the Great". He continued the traditions of the Russian piano school of Anton Rubinstein, Annette Essipova and Vasily Safonov. He taught two outstanding pianists of Russia: Gilels and Richter. The latter acknowledged on many occasions Neuhaus' tremendous influence on him. Besides these two giants of piano, his roster included Yakov Zak, Nathan Perelman, Vera Razumowska, Tatyana Goldfarb, Tamara Guseva, Alexei Nasedkin, Yevgeny Malinin, Anatoly Vedernikov, Oleg Boshniakovich, Lev Naumov and many others. This list would be incomplete without the name of Heinrich's youngest son, Stanislav Neuhaus.

Stanislav was born in Moscow on 21 March, 1927. His mother Zinaida (née Eremeeva, 1897-1966) played the piano from an early age. In 1917 her family moved from St. Petersburg to Elizavetgrad, where she entered the Neuhaus' music school and was taught by Natalie Neuhaus. Heinrich and Zinaida were married in 1918, and soon after moved to Kiev, where Heinrich took a professorship at the Conservatory and Zinaida continued to study piano with him. In 1931 their marriage dissolved. The next year, Zinaida became the wife of the great Russian poet Boris Pasternak. Stanislav remained in her custody and was accepted with love by his stepfather.

Stanislav Neuhaus graduated from the prestigious Gnessin's music school in Moscow in 1941. Among his childhood recollections, the most vivid was one of his father teaching Sviatoslav Richter. The younger Neuhaus remembered: "When I was a boy, I laid down on a bed in my father's apartment and listened to how he taught Slava. Apart from listening, I always watched his hands and thought: 'How clever they are! How well they play everything he performs.' "[8]

Together with the Pasternak family, Stanislav spent the difficult wartime years in the tiny Ural town of Chistopol, where he attended school, worked on the collective farm and occasionally played piano at the night. Upon returning to the capital, the young musician studied at the Moscow Conservatory with Vladimir Belov, the beloved pupil of Felix Blumenfeld, and then with his father.

Stanislav started his concert career at the age of twenty, giving hundreds of performances throughout the USSR. His recitals became highlights, receiving many favourable reviews. In October 1950, a Neuhaus father-son piano duo made its début in Moscow. During the 1950s they toured extensively with programs of Mozart, Chopin, Liszt, Arensky and Rachmaninoff and enjoyed an enthusiastic reception from audiences throughout Russia. In the 1960s and 1970s, Stanislav Neuhaus built his international reputation performing in Western and Eastern European countries and giving master classes in Italy and Austria. His last recital took place in Moscow on January 18th, 1980, one week before his untimely death.

Like his father, Stanislav was a true Russian Romantic. His performances were spontaneous and rhapsodic. Both his playing and his stage appearance were always noble, aristocratic and devoid of excesses. Although Stanislavs's technique lacked a certain virtuoso flair, it was big and solid; he also possessed a unique metric freedom which produced barless song-like phrasing.

Stanislav Neuhaus' performances were uneven. In a bad mood, he could be indifferent and even erratic; but when he was in the right mood, he played with a refined sense of rubato, grace, elegance and great tonal variety.

Like his father, Stanislav specialized in Chopin and Scriabin. His performances of Chopin's two Concerti, Sonatas, Mazurkas, Ballads and Scherzos are still remembered and highly regarded in Russia. With Scriabin, he was flattering, mysterious and ecstatic. Among Scriabin's compositions that he played most often were the Concerto, Sonatas Nos.2,3,4,5 and 9, the Poems and Preludes.

Besides these two pillars, Stanislav's repertoire included Mozart, Beethoven, Liszt, Debussy, Rachmaninoff and Prokofiev. Unfortunately, he did not like recording, and only very few of his records are available now in Russia.

Stanislav Neuhaus joined the Moscow Conservatory in 1957 as his father's assistant and became a full-time professor in 1970. As a teacher, Stanislav followed his father's principles, but modified them in accordance with his own understanding of the teaching process and its goals: compared to Heinrich, Stanislav devoted much more time explaining the "knowhow" of piano-playing rather than discussing broad interpretative aspects of compositions. Neuhaus Junior was meticulously faithful to the original text and was sure to disapprove strongly of any ignorance of its slightest detail. In this regard, he was much less tolerant than his father.

In a classroom, Stanislav was not very talkative and, while teaching, made relatively rare excursions into other arts. His style was more authoritarian than Heinrich's, and he strongly insisted on his own vision and interpretation of compositions played by his students.

To convey a flavour of his teaching, one can quote a few of his statements made in a classroom. Being in the mainstream of "the teaching system" of "Heinrich the Great", they also reflect Stanislav's personality and musical tastes. Here are some of them:

> The musical language is similar to the literary one. The latter consists of sentences and phrases which make sense and constitute narration. No one can read a novel which does not have sentences, periods, commas, etc. Similarly, no one can understand a musical language which does not have the same features. Without them, we hear an inarticulate, chaotic set of sounds rather than true music.

> The degree of "knowhow" distinguishes amateurs from professionals. The latter heavily rely on "knowhow", i.e. on professional skill, while the former count on inspiration, emotions, fantasy and moods.

> My main requirement is rhythm. Any music goes on within a timeframe. This timeframe should be set in such a way that both the pulsation and the breath of the music are felt rather than its metre.

> The sound of the piano is beautiful when it rests on

silence. If at any time of playing you hear a knock, you get mud rather than the clear bright sound.

When playing Chopin, your fingers should be positioned as close to the keyboard as possible. This provides legato and legatissimo, which are so important in his music. On the contrary, when playing Liszt and Scriabin, your fingers should fly above the keyboard like birds.

Playing Romantic composers, especially Chopin, your left hand acts as a conductor while your right hand is a soloist. The latter, being free in expression of various emotions, should follow a conductor. Ideally, both a conductor and a soloist should be equally sensitive to each other.[9]

Among the students whom Stanislav Neuhaus taught either independently or in collaboration with his father were Valery Kastelsky, Yevgeny Mogilevsky, Radu Lupu, Vladimir Kraynev and Georges Andriash. Neither of Stanislav Neuhaus' children chose professional musical careers, and with his early death, the great musical saga of the Neuhaus family came to a close.

Notes

1.   Blumenfeld, Felix, (1863-1931), composer, conductor and
      teacher. He studied piano with Gustav Neuhaus in Elizavetgrad
      in 1875-78; graduated from the St. Petersburg Conservatory
      in 1885. Blumenfeld taught at this Conservatory and became
      its professor in 1911. He was also professor at the Kiev Con-
      servatory (1918-1931). Blumenfeld was a conductor at the
      Mariinski Theatre in St. Petersburg (1895-1911) and conducted
      Russian season's performances in Paris in 1908. He premiered
      many piano compositions by Anatoly Lyadov, Aleksander
      Glazunov and Anton Arensky. Among his students were
      Vladimir Horowitz, Simon Barere, Maria Grinberg, Aleksander
      Dubyansky, Lev Barenboym, and Aleksander Tsfasman.

2.   *Genrikh Neygauz, Vospominaniya, pis'ma, materialy (Heinrich
      Neuhaus. Memoirs, Letters, Materials*, Compiled by Elena
      Richter) IMIDZH, Moscow, 1992, p. 332 (hereafter *Heinrich
      Neuhaus).*

3.   Ibid., p. 31.

4.   Ibid., p. 378.

5.   Anatoly Aleksandrov (1888-1982), composer and teacher.
      Among his compositions: 2 operas, 4 string quartets, 11 sona
      tas for piano, vocal and incidental music. He was awarded the
      Stalin prize in 1951.
       Nikolai Myaskovsky (1887-1950), composer and teacher. He
      studied compositions with A. Lyadov, N. Rimsky-Korsakov and
      R. Glière. Among his compositions are 27 symphonies, 9 string
      quartets, 3 sonatas for piano and vocal music.
      Samuel Feynberg (1890-1962), composer, pianist, teacher. He
      studied piano with A. Goldenweizer and composition with N.
      Zhilyaev and graduated from the Moscow Conservatory in 1911.
      Feynberg was professor at the Moscow Conservatory in 1922-
      62; among his students were Igor Aptekarev, Nina Emelyanova,
      and Leonid Zuzin. His compositions include 3 piano concer
      tos, 12 piano sonatas, numerous suites and fantasies for piano.

Aleksander Kreyn (1883-1951), composer. He studied cello with A. von Glehn and theory with A. Koreshenko, L. Nikolaev and B. Yavorsky and graduated from the Moscow Conservatory in 1908. His compositions include 2 symphonies, several symphonic poems, vocal, piano and incidental music.

6.   *Heinrich Neuhaus,* op. cit., p. 102.

7.   Genrikh, Neygauz. *Ob isskusstve fortepiannoy igry (The Art of Piano Playing).* Muzika, Moscow, 1958.

8.   *Stanislav Neygauz., Vospominaniya, pis'ma, materialy (Stanislav Neuhaus. Memoirs, Letters, Materials,* Compiled by N. Zimjanina), Sovetskiy Kompozitor, Moscow, 1988, p. 78.

9.   Ibid., pp. 148-150.

7

IN THE HISTORY OF PIANO THERE ARE relatively few names of great female concert pianists - Clara Schumann, Arabella Goddard, Sophie Menter, Annette Essipova, Teresa Carreño, Marguerite Long, Myra Hess, Maria Grinberg, Alicia de Larrocha and Martha Argerich. This list would be incomplete without adding the name of one of the greatest Russian pianists of the twentieth century, Maria Yudina.

She was born on the 10th of September, 1899, in the small town of Nevel about 200 miles southwest of St. Petersburg. Her father,

Maria Yudina

Beniamin Yudin, grew up in a large, poor Jewish family. At a very early age, he started working to support his parents. In 1887, he graduated from the medical school of the Moscow University and began work as a physician in Nevel. Very soon, B. Yudin established himself as an excellent specialist, highly respected by his patients. Eventually, he became a prominent public figure in the town through participation in various commissions and advisory committees on public health, education and economic development. Maria inherited the best features of her father's personality - energy, ability to work hard, decisiveness and courage.

The young girl received an excellent education at home, including not only basic subjects but also foreign languages, painting and music. She started to study piano at the age of eight with Frieda Teytelbaum-Levinson, who was a pupil of Anton Rubinstein and the winner of the Rubinstein Prize.

At the age of thirteen, Maria entered the St. Petersburg Conservatory, where she studied with Olga Kalantarova and then with the most famous and capable teacher at that time, Annette Essipova. Unfortunately, Maria's study with Essipova was cut short by her teacher's sudden death in the fall of 1914.

Following the advice of Alexander Glazunov, then the director of the Conservatory, Yudina joined professor Vladimir Drozdov's class, also taking piano lessons with Felix Blumenfeld. In 1917, Yudina dropped her Conservatory studies and came back to Nevel, where she took an active part in the revolutionary movement. Maria returned to the Petrograd (formerly St. Petersburg) Conservatory in 1920 and studied with professor Leonid Nikolaev. Next year, she graduated from the Conservatory with a programme that included compositions by J.S. Bach, Liszt, Beethoven, her classmate Hermann Beak, and Glazunov. As head of the graduation commission, Glazunov commented on Yudina's performance in the following terms: "Yudina is an extremely gifted musician with tremendous musical talent. She demonstrates vivid temperament along with wise and inspired interpretation of lyrical episodes. Her sonority is very colourful... She deserves five-plus."[1] At the graduation ceremony, Maria, together with another graduate, Vladimir Sofronitsky, were awarded the Rubinstein Prize.

The great Russian composer Dmitri Shostakovich, who studied piano and composition in the Petrograd Conservatory at the same time as Yudina, wrote about her: "Yudina was one of my idols. Sometimes I tried to imitate her performing. Later I realized that in doing so I was on a wrong track... However, it was still beneficial for me to imitate such a mature artist as Yudina rather than somebody else of a lower artistic calibre."[2]

Yudina did not restrict her interests to piano-playing. She joined the conducting class of Nicolai Cherepnin and studied organ, percussions and music theory. However, her searching mind was occupied not only by music.

Yudina's deep interest in religion resulted in her conversion to Christianity at the age of nineteen, and she remained a strong believer the rest of her life. In 1921 and 1922, the young pianist attended lectures on history and philosophy at the Petrograd University. Later, Yudina remembered: "I did not become a scientist, because music had already diverted my attention. However, I was happy to acquire the ethical principles on which our existence is based. I gained an access to human knowledge as well as a wide range of subjects for thought."[3]

M. Yudina gave her first recital in the Petrograd Philharmonic Hall in 1922 and in the next year, at the age of 24, she became a professor of the Petrograd Conservatory, the youngest in its history.

During the 1920s, she combined teaching with extensive performance, appearing on concert stages in many cities across the USSR. From the very beginning of her concert career, Yudina expressed keen interest in modern music, much of which was unknown to Russian audiences. Thus, she premiered in Russia Piano Concerti of Nicolai Medtner, Bela Bartók and Paul Hindemith. She also actively promoted compositions of young Leningrad composers such as Vladimir Sherbachev and Aleksander Zhitomirsky.

Such propagation of modern music had been condemned by the Soviet authorities, and in 1930 Yudina was fired from the Conservatory. She moved to the capital of Georgia, Tbilisi, and taught postgraduates in the local Conservatory there. She also gave many recitals in Moscow, Leningrad, Tbilisi, Baku and Yerevan. Some of her concert programs were unusual and intriguing. For instance, in 1934 Yudina gave a recital entitled "The Dance in Piano Music from the Sixteenth Century to Modern Times." This program included a huge repertoire, from pieces by English virginalists to compositions of Yudina's contemporaries.

In 1936, Yudina became a full professor of the Moscow Conservatory, where she taught piano and other musical subjects. She was a very scrupulous teacher, usually working overtime to the verge of emotional exhaustion. She considered sonority and touch to be the main components of the piano technique and worked on them tirelessly with her students.

A brilliantly educated person, Yudina also tried to widen the cultural horizon of young musicians, making them acquainted with classical and modern literature, poetry and the arts. She also strongly believed that knowledge of and adherence to the universal principles of morals and ethics should be an essential component of education, and she introduced these to her students. Needless to say, such a strong emphasis on classical morals and ethics, rather than on orthodox Communist doctrine, was dangerous during the totalitarian Soviet era.

Yudina's approach to students' repertoire was always innovative. She by no means ignored the routine Conservatory curriculum of well-known classical and romantic compositions; yet, despite official censorship and bureaucratic barriers, she also taught her pupils how to play and interpret modern western and Russian music. Very often Yudina played duos and concerti with students at the Conservatory concerts. Her pupils adored her, especially the female ones, who often imitated not only their teacher's performing style but also her dresses, walk and mannerisms.

Yudina spent the war years in Moscow. In the summer of 1941, when the war between Russia and Germany erupted, she entered the nursing-school and upon graduation applied for a post in the Field Forces. Fortunately, her application was rejected, and she started to work as a night nurse in the Moscow military hospital. At the same time, she continued teaching at the Moscow Conservatory and broadcast many programs for servicemen at the front. She did not stop broadcasting even in December 1941, during the critical German assault on the Russian capital. In response to her playing, she received many letters from soldiers and officers who expressed their thanks for her support and encouragement. This is one of them: "We have listened to your performance of Beethoven's Fantasy and approved it. Thank you. We want to assure you that we shall defend Soviet culture and you. Privates Antonov and Terentiev, snipers."[3]

In 1941 and 1942, Yudina continued supporting the war effort by giving several fundraising concerti in Moscow. In February of 1943, when almost half of European Russia was occupied by German troops, Yudina flew to besieged Leningrad to give a recital.

In 1951, Yudina quit the Moscow Conservatory and joined the Moscow Gnessin Institute of Music. In the 1950s and 1960s, she made many appearances throughout the USSR, performing in Russia, Siberia, Ukraine and the Baltic republics, where her concerts were always packed. Yudina also made two concert tours abroad. In 1950, she performed in the former German Democratic Republic in connection with the bicentennial of Bach's death. Upon her arrival in Leipzig, Yudina walked barefoot from the terminal to the composer's grave at St. Thomas' church to express her admiration for him.

She also gave a few concerts in Poland in 1954. Unfortunately, the Soviet authorities never allowed her to cross the "Iron Curtain", and for a long time the West remained unfamiliar with this brilliant and original performer.

During her later years, some of Yudina's concerts had a particular subject. In 1955 she gave a series of five recitals entitled "Selected Piano Sonatas", which included 22 Sonatas of various composers from D. Scarlatti to D. Shostakovich. The titles of some of Yudina's concert series of the 1960s - such as "Romanticism, Its Sources and Parallels", or "A Man and Nature" - speak for themselves. Being a great admirer of Stravinsky, she performed many of his piano and chamber compositions in 1962 to commemorate his 80th birthday.

In the last decade of her life, Yudina produced numerous recordings of Beethoven, Mussorgsky, Berg, Bartók, Hindemith and Jolivet. Many of these are still unknown in the West, awaiting re-issue on CD.

M. Yudina passed away in Moscow on 19 November, 1970.

Her performing style was inspiring and majestic, recalling human speech with all its nuances, ranging from pathetics to intimacy. Her repertoire and interpretations had a personal stamp which reflected her personality. In her interpretations, Yudina worked down from "the large picture", which could be inspired by some *a priori* idea, and emphasized specific details of music to support it. If her "large picture" fit the composer's conception and expressiveness, the result was astonishing. If it did not, her performance could be less convincing but still remained intriguing.

Professor Samary Savshinsky of the Leningrad Conservatory once recalled:

> I went to the concert where Yudina played 32 Variations by Beethoven. Her interpretation of this piece seemed strange to me. After the concert I rushed backstage and Yudina asked me: "How did it go?" "Well, Maria, I didn't understand it." "How come?" she replied indignantly. "Did you realize that it was *The Tempest* by Shakespeare?" Then she approached pi-

ano and again played a few variations. "This is Caliban, this is Prospero, and this is Alonso," she explained to me in the course of playing. To be honest, I didn't understand the overall interpretation any better after this explanation.[4]

Yudina was on her home ground performing Baroque composers, from J.S. Bach's predecessors to W. Mozart. She was one of the very few pianists who played in concerts both volumes of Bach's *Well-Tempered Clavier*. She had an affinity with Beethoven: Yudina played his 3rd, 4th and 5th Piano Concerti, the 32 Variations, the 33 Variations on a Waltz by Diabelli, the Variations and Fugue (*Eroica* Variations), the Fantasy for piano, choir and orchestra, many sonatas and chamber music. In particular, her performance of Beethoven's Piano Concerto No.4 was unforgettable. When Yudina played its second movement, Adagio, time seemed to stop and listeners were plunged into sublime meditation.

Heinrich Neuhaus once said that Yudina's rendition of the late Beethoven Sonatas demonstrated "the feast of mind and the orgy of intellect." Playing Sonatas Nos. 31 and 32, she perfectly shaped their symphonic scope and devoted herself entirely to the philosophical depth of these masterpieces.

Yudina seldom played the Romantic music of Chopin, Liszt, Schubert and Schumann. This deep-thinking artist preferred philosophical reflections and intellectual search to openly expressed emotions. For this reason her favourite Russian composers were Taneev and Medtner rather than Tchaikovsky and Rachmaninoff. Of North American pianists, perhaps, Glenn Gould most resembles Yudina in this spirit and attitude.

Together with Sviatoslav Richter, Yudina was among the top interpreters of M. Mussorgsky's *Pictures at an Exhibition*. She expressed profound thoughts on its interpretation in a brilliantly written essay entitled "Modest Petrovich Mussorgsky: *Pictures at an Exhibition*" completed in 1970, a few months before her death, and published in 1974.[5]

Yudina was the unquestionable champion of performing modern western music in the USSR. It would be difficult to name any reasonably significant modern composer whose compositions she had not played. Despite strict government censorship, she made her audiences familiar with piano music of Schoenberg, Berg, Hindemith, Honegger,

Jolivet, Milhaud, Messiaen, Poulenc, Martinu, Bartók, Barber and Stravinsky. Many young Soviet composers, including those who were not recognized by the Soviet musical establishment, were indebted to Yudina for her public performances of their compositions.

As the leading Russian musicologist on Yudina, Anatoly Kuznetsov pointed out her struggle with the Soviet authorities for performances of new music by both Russian and western composers. She was also a great interpreter of her contemporaries, Prokofiev and Shostakovich. Following the première of Prokofiev's Piano Concerto No. 2, played by the composer, Yudina was the second pianist to perform it, in the fall of 1933 in Kiev. Although her interpretation significantly differed from Prokofiev's own, the composer publicly and privately praised her rendition. In 1935, he presented Yudina with one of his piano miniatures, with the following inscription: "In memory of your performance of my Second Piano Concerto."

Yudina enjoyed chamber music and played it often. Her collaboration with the Beethoven Quartet was very fruitful and lasted for many years. They played a huge and diverse repertoire together, including compositions of Beethoven, Brahms, Schubert, Glinka, Borodin, Taneev and Shostakovich. Of special interest was their performance of the Taneev's majestic Quintet, in which Yudina as pianist demonstrated exceptional richness and diversity of sonority and a deep penetration into the philosophical nature of Taneev's masterpiece.

While Yudina was never involved in politics, her independent and openly expressed opinions on many fundamental problems, and her faith in strong moral and religious principles contradicted the norms of life in totalitarian USSR. One episode can give an example of Yudina's independent and strong character. It is well known that Stalin often listened to the radio. One day, he called the Broadcast Committee, requesting a record of Mozart's Piano Concerto No. 23, which Yudina had played the day before. No recording had been made during this live performance, but, to comply with Stalin's request, both Yudina and the entire symphony were called in and they recorded the concert at night. One single copy was produced and sent to Stalin. Shortly after Yudina received an envelope from the Kremlin containing twenty thousand rubles. In response she wrote to the dictator who had tried to destroy religious life in Russia: "I thank you, Josef Vissarionovich, for your aid. I will pray for you day and night and ask the Lord to forgive your great sins before the people and the country. The Lord is merciful and He will forgive you. I gave the money to the church that I attend."[6] Everybody expected the worst to happen to Yudina, but fortunately, no punishment followed.

Of Yudina, something should be said of her profound inner life and unique personality. She lived in a spiritually charged environment. Among her close friends were such outstanding figures as the philosopher Michail Bachtin, the poet Boris Pasternak, the religious thinker Father Pavel Florensky, who died in a labour camp, the painters Vladimir Favorsky and Pavel Korin, the poet Nicolai Zabolotsky, imprisoned for several years, and the architect Victor Vesnin. It is interesting to note that one of the first readings of the unfinished novel *Doctor Zhivago* took place in Yudina's Moscow apartment in 1947.

There is an interesting link between Yudina and Pasternak's family. While in Moscow in the 1930s, Maria was a frequent guest of Boris Pasternak's first wife Yevgeniya Lur'e. In her modest one bedroom apartment one piece of furniture stood out from the others: it was a beautiful grand Bechstein, on which Yudina liked to play for hours. This instrument had been bought in Germany almost fifty years ago by Boris' mother, Rosalia Isidorovna Pasternak, who had brought it to Moscow.

Music and Christianity were the two pillars in Yudina's life. Yudina sent money and clothes to exiled and imprisoned friends and unknown people. She also supported both morally and financially many families of victims of Stalin's repression, including the widow and children of Father Florensky.

Despite an eruptive temper, Yudina was nevertheless extremely tolerant of human deficiencies and weaknesses. She once said: "Let us take courage from compassion... Let us be dissolved in other people."[7]

Yudina paid a high price for her intellectual and artistic independence. She was fired from the Leningrad Conservatory and forced to quit the Moscow Conservatory. Her domestic life was unsettled and uncomfortable, to say the least. She sacrificed both her material well-being and her private life to fulfil her artistic mission.

One of the greatest modern composers, Karlheinz Stockhausen, once said of Yudina: "Maria Yudina and her like are artists in the true sense of this word. They are able to receive signals from the remote sources... For eternity a single human life does not normally mean too much, but that does not hold where a great artist is concerned. Yudina was extremely sensitive to the future; she was a courageous person with a wonderful and ardent heart."[8]

Notes:

1. Yudina, Maria Veniaminovna *Stat'i, vospominaniya, materialy* (*M.V. Yudina. Articles, Memoirs, Materials.* Compiled by Anatoly Kuznetsov.), Sovetskiy Kompozitor, Moscow, 1978, p.189

2. Ibid., p. 41.

3. Ibid., p. 219.

4. Ibid., p. 43.

5. Yudina, M., "Modest Petrovich Musorgskiy: Kartinki svystavki" ("Modest Petrovich Mussorgsky: Pictures at an Exhibition"), *Sovetskaya muzika* (*The Soviet Music Magazine*), No. 9, 1974.

6. *Testimony: The Memoirs of Dmitri Shostakovich* as related to and edited by S.Volkov. Limelight Editions, New York, 1979, p. 194.

7. Kuznetsov, A., "Maria Yudina. Iz vospominaniy." *Novy mir,* No. 6, 1997, p. 240.7

8. *Yudina,* M., op. cit., p. 23.

THE FAITHFUL PERFECTIONIST

On December 21ˢᵀ, 1992, in London, one of the twentieth century's greatest violinists, Nathan Milstein died at the age of eighty-nine. He was the last among the legendary violinists that included Mischa Elman, Miron Polyakin, Jascha Heifetz, Efrem Zimbalist and David Oistrakh. They were all born before the 1917 Revolution on the peripheries of the Russian Empire, achieved great fame, and made a significant contribution to the art of the violin.

Nathan Milstein was born on December 31ˢᵗ, 1903, in Odessa, a prosperous port on the Black Sea with Russian, Ukrainian, and Jewish communities that contributed immensely to a flourishing musical life. The city featured numerous musical societies, salons, concert halls, and music schools, as well as a famous opera house and a high-level conservatory. Sounds of piano or violin music emanated from both the luxurious homes of the rich and the dark basements of the poor. Nathan's father Miron was a merchant who made his wealth importing wool and fabric from Poland and England to Russia. As a young boy, Nathan revealed restlessness and an inclination to risky pranks; so to discipline his impetuous character, his parents decided that he should study the violin. Initially, Nathan studied with a private teacher, but soon he entered the music school directed by Pyotr Stolyarsky which was dubbed "a factory of talents". Among Stolyarsky's pupils were such outstanding violinists as Samuel Furer, David Oistrakh, Elizabeth Gilels, Boris and Michail Goldstein, Michail Fikhtengolz, Aleksander Livont, and Arthur Zisserman.

According to his contemporaries, Stolyarsky was an ordinary performer, but he possessed an enormous pedagogical gift. From the dozens of children attending his school, he was able to pick out and give special attention to those who had a real potential to become outstanding violinists. He knew how to inspire and maintain children's interest in music, and, what is equally important, he knew "the secret" of how to transform routine technical development into challenging and exciting everyday work. Stolyarsky preferred group lessons to individual ones, and such a group usually consisted of ten to fifteen children playing in unison. During these lessons, pupils' younger brothers and sisters would be playing toys and games on the floor in Stolyarsky's studio, creating quite a noisy environment. This, however, did not bother either young violinists or their teacher.

Besides these group lessons, the most gifted pupils studied with Stolyarsky individually and often each of them had several short lessons every day.

Stolyarsky taught Nathan for almost two years. Under his guidance the young musician acquired a solid technique and a vast repertoire, which included a few violin concerti.

At the age of nine Nathan made his first public appearance, playing the Concerto for violin by Aleksander Glazunov with the Odessa Symphony. The venerable composer, who conducted the Symphony, was very pleased with Nathan's rendition of his composition.

In 1915, Leopold Auer, professor at the St. Petersburg Conservatory, heard Nathan's playing in Odessa and invited the young violinist to come to the capital and study with. Accompanied by his mother, Nathan moved to St. Petersburg, and without any formality, was accepted at the oldest and best Russian musical institution. However, one difficulty arose upon the Milsteins' arrival in the city: as a Jew, Maria did not have permission to live in the Russian capital. It required the direct interference of Glazunov, who called the Deputy Minister of the Interior and resolved this delicate problem. Soon after arrival, the young musician gave his first recital in the capital.

Later on Milstein reminisced on this public performance:

> He (Auer) said, "You will not get anything, but it will
> be very good for you to play." I got twenty five rubles,
> a box of chocolates - and applause. I thought, this is
> the best profession.[1]

At that time Auer's class was a unique assembly of prodigies, including Jascha Heifetz, Miron Polyakin and Tosha Seidel. Nathan not only heard their playing almost daily, but also performed in front of them during his studies with Auer.

Much later, when he became a famous musician, Milstein emphasized on many occasions that the role of a teacher in the musical development of a gifted student is usually exaggerated, and neither Stolyarsky nor Auer significantly influenced him. However, Nathan remembered at least some of Auer's pedagogical instructions for the rest of his life and applied them in his practice. In particular, Auer persistently told Nathan: "A piece should be learned by the head rather than by fingers." This terse advice meant that intellect should always prevail over technique and the overall interpretative concept should define the performance details.

Almost immediately after the 1917 Revolution, Auer left Russia and emigrated first to Norway and then to the USA. With his departure from St. Petersburg, Nathan's musical education was over. Many years later, as a mature musician looking back at the beginning of his career, Milstein stated that such an early completion of his formal musical training, at the age of fourteen, had been beneficial to him. In particular, it had encouraged his self-perfection and prevented him from copying his classmates and teacher.

The 1917 Revolution ruined Miron Milstein's business and brought severe hardship on his family. To make a living and support his parents, Nathan was pushed to perform intensively. Together with his sister Sara, who was an accomplished pianist, he played in Odessa and many Ukrainian cities, enjoying enthusiastic acceptance from the audiences. In the winter of 1921, while playing a series of concerts in Kiev, Milstein met Vladimir Horowitz.

I had never met Vladimir Horowitz... At my Kiev concert the accompanist was Sergei Tarnovsky, who at that
time was Horowitz' teacher. Through him Horowitz,
with his sister Regina, came to hear me and came back-
stage at the end... He said: "My father and mother in-
vite you to come to tea." I went and at tea there were
some professors, among them Heinrich Neuhaus.
During tea, we grew tired of our elders' talk. Anybody
over thirty was old to us then! And Regina, who was a
pianist like her brother, said: "Come to my room. I
have a piano there." She played Chopin and Schumann.
Then Horowitz played Puccini and Wagner, his own
piano arrangements of operas... Time flew by. Volodya's
mother came in. "Children, dinner is served." After
we had eaten, we continued to make music. Volodya
and I played sonatas and he accompanied me in concerti.
It grew so late that I was asked to spend the night. We
slept four in the same room, Papa, Volodya, his brother,
and me... The next morning, when I woke up I was
asked to stay on. I had come for tea and stayed for
three years.[2]

From 1921 to 1925, both musicians toured almost non-stop through
Ukraine, Belorussia, Georgia, Azerbaijan and Russia. Their typical joint
recital consisted of three parts: starting with Milstein playing solo, then
it was Horowitz' turn, and eventually playing violin sonatas of César
Franck, Edward Grieg, and Camille Saint-Saëns together.

In the fall of 1923, Milstein and Horowitz made their début in
Moscow and Petrograd (formerly St. Petersburg). At the Moscow concert on 21 October, the young musicians presented the Russian premières
of S. Prokofiev's Violin Concerto No. 1 and Szymanowski's Violin
Concerto No. 1. They repeated this performance in Petrograd. The music
reviewer of the Petrograd *Krasnaya gazeta* (*The Red Newspaper*) wrote:
"Playing only Prokofiev and Szymanowski through the whole evening
requires courage... It is a pity that both composers were unable to attend
their premières; it is most unlikely that they could hear a better performance."[3]

The leading Russian music critic of the time, Vyacheslav Karatygin, pointed out that "Horowitz and Milstein are young artists full of youthful ardor, boiling passions, tempestuous agitation and temperament."[4]

A most important and ecstatic review of the musicians' Moscow début entitled "Children of the Soviet Revolution" appeared in the government newspaper *Izvestia* (*News*) and was signed by Anatoly Lunacharsky, the People's Commissar of Education in the Soviet government. This review brought Horowitz and Milstein many invitations to play at high-ranking Communist Party meetings and rallies. At one of these events they were introduced to Ieronim Uborevich, the Deputy of the People's Military Commissar - Leon Trotsky. Uborevich was so pleased with their performance that he suggested Milstein and Horowitz should go on a concert tour abroad to demonstrate the cultural achievements of the Soviet Russia to the West. Using his power, the Deputy procured an official mandate "for the purpose of artistic refinement and cultural propaganda," which allowed both musicians to stay in Europe for two years.

At the end of 1925, Milstein left Russia and moved to Germany. Although the violinist's name was unknown to German audiences, his concerts in Berlin and Hamburg were quite successful. In 1926, he moved to Paris and decided to complete his musical education with the Belgian violinist Eugène Ysaÿe. Many years later Milstein remembered his first meeting with this great musician:

I went to see him at the resort town of Zout sur Mer - on the coast not far from Ostend... I came to Ysaÿe without an appointment, afraid that if I tried to set a date, his secretary would tell me to stay home and not bother the maestro. I spent my last centime on the trip. When I reached La Chanterelle, Ysaÿe's secretary came out to see me. As I later learned, Jeanette, an American from Brooklyn, was his former student. Ysaÿe would marry her shortly.

Jeanette was stern with me: "*Le maître* is tired, he is resting. He cannot see you!" I pleaded, explaining that I didn't have money to return. We argued for a while. Suddenly Ysaÿe came out, enormous and completely naked. "What's all this noise?" He really had been taking a nap, after the beach. Our arguing had awakened him.

"What's the problem?"

"Some kid wants to play for you..."

"Why not? If he's bad, we'll send him home."

Even when roused from sleep, Ysaÿe was reasonable. He led me inside and threw on a beach robe, which barely covered his bulging flesh...

Sitting down, Ysaÿe asked, "What will you play?"

"What would you like to hear, Maestro?"

"A Paganini caprice!"

With extreme modesty, I said, "Maestro, which one of the twenty-four would you prefer?" Ysaÿe asked for the first caprice, a rather difficult one. I delivered. He asked for the last one, the twenty-fourth (also not easy). Ysaÿe didn't hear it through. He interrupted me and asked, "What do you play of Bach?" When I offered him a choice here, too, Ysaÿe didn't believe his ears! Skeptically, he had me play the Fugue from the First Sonata. I won't say that I performed it well, but I was getting through it, when Ysaÿe interrupted me again.

"Why so fast?"

"Would you like it slower, Maestro?"

Ysaÿe said hurriedly, "No." Then he said, "Listen, my child, what do you need here? You play Paganini well, Bach, too. What more do you want?" The praise was nice, but I was also disappointed: *the maître* was sending me home! Noticing my saddened face, Ysaÿe took pity. "You know what, my child, come to my house tonight. We'll play some chamber music."[5]

During the next several months Milstein and Ysaÿe played a lot of chamber music. At one of these evenings Nathan was introduced to Queen Elizabeth of Belgium, an amateur violinist, who became his friend and the admirer of his talent for many years to come. Although Milstein never overestimated Her Majesty's musical gift, he highly respected her for her deep devotion to musicians and classical music.

After a few months in Belgium, Milstein returned to Paris. During the next three years he played as a soloist and as a member of a trio throughout Europe and South America, together with Horowitz and Gregor Piatigorsky,. The three young, energetic and successful musicians from Russia were dubbed as "Three Musketeers".

On 29 October, 1929, Milstein made his North American début in Philadelphia, playing the Violin Concerto by Glazunov with the Philadelphia Symphony under the baton of Leopold Stokovski.

In 1931 in New York, the violinist was introduced to Sergei Rachmaninoff. Milstein reminisced on him:

> I met him in 1931, when I was twenty-seven. We were introduced by my old Odessa friend Oskar von Riesemann, with whom I became reacquainted when I arrived in Switzerland... Once, I was performing in Lucerne and Riesemann brought Rachmaninoff, his wife, their daughter Tatyana, and Tatyana's husband, Boris Conus...
>
> At that concert, I played the Bach E major Partita for solo violin, and apparently my performance acted as an impulse for Rachmaninoff to do a wonderful piano transcription of some of the movements - the Prelude, the Gavotte, and the Gigue - which he subsequently published as a suite.
>
> Then came the day when Rachmaninoff said to me, "Nathan Mironovich, I'm giving a conert in Paris. I'll be playing the Bach Prelude in my transcription for the first time there. You come hear it. And in the intermission, tell me your opinion..."
>
> I went to the concert and listened attentively, all ears. There was one passage in the transcription of the Prelude that I didn't like; I didn't think it sounded "Bachian" enough.
>
> After the first part of the concert, I went back to see Rachmaninoff, as he had requested, and now I was afraid! Afraid to tell the truth. But I just couldn't not tell it. Only what should I say? I made abashful face and began, "Sergei Vasilyevich, I have some doubts: in the Prelude, it seems to me, you have a chromatic sequence, which doesn't sound just right" - Rachmaninoff interrupted angrily, "Go to hell!"
>
> Oh boy, I thought, this is coming to a bad end for me. Of course, going to hell was not obligatory, but staying around Rachmaninoff was uncomfortable. There was the distinct possibility of a scene...

After the concert Rachmaninoff's daughter was giving a dinner party. I didn't know whether to go. My God, Rachmaninoff was going to hate me now! His wife, Natalia Aleksandrovna, saw me still at the theatre, clearly in despair, and came over to me. "Do come with us. Sergei Vasilyevich didn't mean to offend you. He was just nervous after performing." I went, feeling as if I were headed for the guillotine or for questioning by the Soviet Cheka (secret police –E.Z.). When I got to their house, I stayed in a corner, fearing Rachmaninoff's wrath.

His friends were all there: the composers Glazunov, Medtner, Grechaninov, and Julius Conus (father of Boris). Rachmaninoff still seemed to be in a huff at first, but then, after dinner, he called me into the library: "Nathan Mironovich, come along, come along!" I felt resurrected!

In the library a discussion began, with Rachmaninoff asking Glazunov: "Sasha, did you hear any clumsy chromatic sequences in my Bach transcription?" Apparently Glazunov had not listened too closely during the concert. No, Glazunov hadn't heard anything like that. Then Rachmaninoff turned to Medtner. "Nika, did you?" But Medtner must have been thinking about the dinner and wine to come after the concert. He hadn't noticed either. So I had been the only interested listener! And I knew that Partita well from my own playing.

Still, I saw that Rachmaninoff was no longer angry with me, and no longer wished me to go to hell. I was pleased. After dinner I went to my room at the Hotel Majestic on Avenue Kleber - Rachmaninoff was staying there too. When I returned, the concierge stopped me. "M. Rachmaninoff would like you to go to his suite."

> I was afraid: what if he cursed me again? I meekly
> opened the door to his suite - just a tiny bit, not daring
> to enter - and he shouted, "Come in, come in! You
> were right!" I was ecstatic![6]

Rachmaninoff's appreciation of Milstein's musicianship is also seen
from the following little-known fact: in 1934, before the first performance of *The Rhapsody on a Theme of Paganini*, Op. 43, the composer
sent its score to Milstein, asking him to make the bowing comfortable
for strings to play. It was a great pleasure for Nathan to do it on behalf
of his friend Rachmaninoff.

Milstein became an American citizen in 1942. Three years later, he
married Theresa Kauffman, with whom he had one child, their daughter, Maria.

In the 1940s, the violinist's performing style gradually changed.
His energy and demonstration of tremendous technique were replaced
by a refined artistry, nobility and deepened interpretation. After World
War II, Milstein moved to London, from where he continued to give
concerts throughout the world. By that time, he had an enormous repertoire of baroque, classical and romantic works. He gravitated towards
large-scale compositions, frequently playing violin concerti by Bach,
Vivaldi, Mozart, Paganini, Wieniawski, Beethoven, Mendelssohn, Brahms,
Tchaikovsky, Dvořák, Bruch, Saint-Saëns, Szymanowski, Glazunov,
Prokofiev, Stravinsky, and Berg. However, his repertoire was not comprehensive and clearly reflected his personal taste and passions. Thus
Milstein performed practically no modern composers, and almost
everything composed after World War II was beyond his interest. He
explained this in an interview:

> People don't know how to write for the violin any more.
> There was never in musical history such a universal lack
> of quality. The connection between Beethoven,
> Schubert, Schumann, Brahms, and Wagner is continu-
> ous like a chain reaction. There was not even a pause;
> from Rimsky-Korsakov, the Russian school and French
> school, and their intermarriage and influence, you had
> Stravinsky, who started to write in the nineteenth cen-
> tury. Prokofiev wrote his best works when he was nine-
> teen, before World War I, Stravinsky, Bartók, Berg. Fin-

ish! That was all written forty-five years ago. Now you
have cement music, concrete music, electronic music.
Atonal music is a destruction... If you ask me who made
the greatest contribution to music, I would say: Bach,
Beethoven, Mozart, Haydn, Schubert, Schumann...[7]

Milstein's main achievement was performing and recording the complete Bach's Sonatas and Partitas for solo violin. The first recording was
made in 1956, but it did not satisfy the violinist. The second recording
was done by Deutsche Grammophon in 1976. It received many awards,
including a Grammy from the National Academy of Recording Arts
and Sciences and the Diplome d'Honneur at the Montreaux International Awards and is still considered a standard in solo Bach recordings.

Even when playing the great Romantics, Milstein avoided excessive
rubato and excessive expressiveness. His performance was always elegant, intellectual, well balanced and refined with regard to the compositions' structure and style. Speaking of the refinement and nobility of
Milstein's performance, the music critic Estelle Kerner called him "a
brahmin with violin."[8]

Milstein did not like to produce a large sound. He followed and
cherished what Ysaÿe told him once: "Never play classical music (including baroque and Mozart) *forte-fortissimo*. Remember: *forte* simply means, "*don't play piano*", and if it says *piano*, "don't play *forte*."[9]

Milstein possessed a penetrating "silvery" tone that immediately
distinguished his playing from that of any other violinist. His enormous technique seemed innate and was polished to perfection at a very
early age. This allowed him to concentrate his efforts on the style and
interpretation of the compositions he performed.

Over his long artistic life Milstein played with all the leading con-
ductors of the time, including such towering figures as Arturo Toscanini,
Wilhelm Furtwängler, Karl Muck, Leopold Stokovski, Herbert von
Karajan, Piere Monteux, Eugene Ormandy, Dmitri Mitropolous, George
Szell, and Daniel Barenboim. Although he highly respected and even
admired some of them, especially Toscanini, his general attitude towards
the caste of conductors was quite skeptical. Speaking on this subject,
Milstein once said:

People say so-and-so is a great conductor. He cannot
be great at twenty-five. A conductor is an artist, a great

personality who can *teach* the orchestra - that is *a conductor.* But today nobody can. Since you only need yourself to be a great violinist, pianist, cellist, singer, you can experiment. You are completely in the music, *you make music.* Conductors do not make music. They make somebody else play. I made recordings, and when it came through, it was because I said something, not the conductor. Very often I stop the conductor and tell the orchestra how to do it.[10]

In another interview Milstein again talked on conducting:

I do not want to be a conductor but once I would like the chance to conduct and bring out my own point of view. I would like to prepare the orchestra the way a theater director, an Olivier or a Stanislavsky, prepares a play. I would train and encourage the musicians the way a director does his actors. Then when the concert comes I would step aside... The orchestra would play alone. At the first performance the men might be bashful. But soon they would lose their inhibitions. They would begin to feel free, to put in their own pepper and salt and Heinz Ketchup... The orchestra could become like one great soloist.[11]

Interestingly enough, this is exactly the way *Persimfans*, founded by another pupil of Auer, Lev Tseitlin, performed in Moscow in the 1920s and 1930s - the "symphony without a conductor".

Conductors were much more complementary to Milstein than he to them. Daniel Barenboim remembered:

Nathan Milstein...played with me very often during my years in Paris. He was able to produce the most individual and beautiful sound in the most effortless way imaginable... Milstein's great lesson to me as a conductor and, I suppose, to many violinists, is that one should never force the violin and never try to go beyond the limit of volume and intensity than the instrument can take or provide... There were occasions in Paris when we would play the Mendelssohn or the Brahms Violin Concerto several times in one week and I was amazed by his gift of improvisation, changing fingerings and bowings from one evening to the next naturally and effortlessly. Milstein has remained for me the supreme example of the pure violinist.[12]

After World War II, Milstein became engaged in teaching and held master classes at the famous Juilliard School of Music in New York and for the Foundation for International Master Classes in Music in Zurich. Although some of his students were quite talented, none have become internationally known. Milstein also composed for the violin. Among his compositions are *Paganiniana* for solo violin, based on themes from *Twenty-Four Caprices* by N. Paganini, cadenzi to Violin Concerti by Beethoven and Brahms, and a transcription for solo violin of Liszt's *Mephisto Waltz* No. I.

Although music was the main focus of his life, Milstein had interests in many other fields. He was a great fan of Russian literature and Aleksander Pushkin, Nikolai Gogol, Leo Tolstoy, Anton Chekhov and Leonid Andreyev were among his favourite writers. He was also an art collector of a highly cultivated taste, and his collection of paintings included several masterpieces of distinguished French artists. Milstein himself was an accomplished amateur painter, not only presenting his own drawings and watercolors to friends, but also participating in a few exhibitions. One of them was held in the Metropolitan Museum of Art in New York and consisted only of paintings of musicians. Among its participants were Arnold Schoenberg, George Gershwin and the singer Lotte Lehmann. To the great delight to Milstein, his watercolor *Petersburg in May* was sold for five hundred dollars.

Milstein was a handsome man, and his stage appearance was always elegant and natural. One should agree with Boris Schwarz that "attending a Milstein's performance is an aesthetic as well as a musical experience."[13]

The musician was elegant and aristocratic in his private life as well: he liked fashionable clothes, cozy restaurants with delicious food, fast cars, luxurious hotels, elite spas. Among his friends were members of royal families, influential politicians, brilliant intellectuals and outstanding musicians and artists. However, despite these powerful surroundings, Milstein always maintained his own independent view on various issues, including arts and politics. Without becoming involved in politics, Milstein expressed openly in interviews and private conversations with Soviet musicians his negative attitude towards the lack of freedom and democracy in the USSR. On these grounds, he insistently rejected all invitations to make concert tours through the USSR, even during the Gorbachev era.

Like several of his contemporaries such as Leopold Stokovski, Arthur Rubinstein and Pablo Casals, Nathan Milstein demonstrated exceptional artistic longevity. In 1979, the fiftieth anniversary of Milstein's North American début and his seventy-fifth birthday were widely celebrated in the USA. The hero of the day gave several recitals and played with the leading American symphonies. He continued to give concerts until the last months of his life.

Milstein was awarded many decorations, including Officer and Commander of the French Legion of Honour, the Austrian *Ehrenkruez* and the American Kennedy Centre Award. He was a member of the Academy of Santa Cecilia in Rome. For more than seven decades Milstein's playing was admired by both international audiences and his fellow violinists; his recordings are still considered definitive by many.

Notes:

1.   Kerner, Estelle, "Nathan Milstein Brahmin with Violin", *High Fidelity Magazine*, November 1977: 84-88 (hereafter Kerner).

2.   Soria, Dorle , "Artistic Life". *High Fidelity/Musical America*, July 1974: 7-9 (hereafter Soria).

3.   *Krasnaya gazeta (The Red Newspaper)*, Petrograd, December 8, 1923.

4.   Karatygin, Vyacheslav,   "Semper idem". *Zhis'n iskusstva (The Life of Art)*, Petrograd, 1923, No. 51.

5.   Milstein, Nathan and Volkov., Solomon, *From Russia to the West*, Henry Holt and Company, New York, 1990, pp. 96-97 (here after *From Russia*).

6.   Ibid., pp. 109-111.

7.   Kerner, op. cit., p. 88.

8.   See note 3.

9.   *From Russia to the West*, op. cit., p. 101.

10.   Kerner, p. 88.

11.   Soria, op. cit., p. 9.

12   Barenboim, Daniel, *A Life in Music*, Weindenfeld and Nicolson, London, 1991, p. 108.

13.   Schwarz., Boris, *Great Masters of the Violin*, Simon Schuster, Inc., New York, 1983, pp. 442-446.

FIRST VIOLIN OF RUSSIA

SEPTEMBER 30TH, 1908, IN ODESSA, Ukraine. His mother was a chorister at the Odessa Opera Theatre. His stepfather, whom David always called father, was a street vendor, an amateur violin and wind-instrument player. As a prisoner of World War I, he used his musical talent and played in the prisoners' band.

David remembered of his childhood:

> I was three and a half years old when my father brought to me a toy violin. "Playing" it, I pretended to be a street musician...
> It seemed to me that I would be a happiest person if I went with my violin from one backyard to another to play. I was so carried away by this game that, when at the age of five I got a real small violin and started music lessons, this activity completely absorbed me.[1]

Oistrakh's first and only teacher was the legendary Pyotr Stolyarsky; David entered his school at the age of five.

In 1914, he made his first public appearance, playing in a concert of Stolyarsky's students. It is interesting to note that Nathan Milstein, four years senior to David, performed his graduation program at the same concert.

In 1923, David entered Stolyarsky's class at the Odessa Conservatory. The next year, he performed the Concerto in A minor by J.S. Bach with the Conservatory String Orchestra.

Oistrakh graduated from the Conservatory in 1926. His graduation program included Prokofiev's Concerto No. I, Op. 19, which was still a novelty at that time, the *Devil's Trill* Sonata by Tartini, *Passacaglia* by Handel, and Anton Rubinstein's rarely performed Sonata for viola and piano. Oistrakh remembered of this graduation: "At that time I played fluently and with purity of intonation. However, I needed much more hard work on quality, rhythm, dynamics and, most important, interpretation." [2]

In the fall of 1927, the young violinist performed Glazunov's Concerto Op. 82 in Kiev and Odessa under the composer's direction. In Oistrakh's archive there is a score of this Concerto with the following hand-written dedication: "To the highly talented young virtuoso and artist David Oistrakh in memory of our concerts in Ukraine. From a sincerely devoted admirer of his gift, A. Glazunov. November 17, 1927." [3]

In 1928 Nicolai Malko, chief conductor of the Leningrad Philharmonic, was on tour in Odessa. After hearing Oistrakh's performance of an arrangement of Claude Debussy's *Doll's Serenade*, he told the violinist: "Young man, you are too old to play with dolls and not old enough to sing serenades." [4]

Malko invited David to play with his orchestra at the opening of the next concert season in Leningrad. The Leningrad début took place on October 10th, 1928, when Oistrakh performed Tchaikovsky's Concerto Op. 35 with the famous Leningrad Philharmonic conducted by Malko. The concert was a success and the soloist recieved favourable reviews in local newspapers.

Encouraged by this début, David left Odessa and moved to Moscow at the end of 1928. His first years in the capital were difficult ones. He did not have a permanent position and to make a living, had to take any musical job available. Thus, he participated in light entertainment concerts and played as an accompanist and on-call violinist. With a group of artists, David often toured various cities and townships, spending nights in railway stations or in uncomfortable guest houses.

In 1930, Oistrakh married a young pianist, Tamara Rotareva, who had recently graduated from the Odessa Conservatory. It is interesting to note that her Conservatory teacher was Theophile Richter, the father of great pianist-to-be Sviatoslav Richter. In 1931, Tamara gave birth to their son Igor, who later became a distinguished violinist in his own right.

In Moscow, Oistrakh became acquainted with such outstanding musicians as Konstantin Igumnov, Heinrich Neuhaus, Miron Polyakin, and Vladimir Sofronitsky. He also established a relationship with famous violin teachers and professors at the Moscow Conservatory - Abram Yampolsky, Lev Tseitlin and Konstantin Mostras - and they significantly widened his musical horizon.

On January 22nd, 1929, Oistrakh gave his first Moscow recital, playing a mixture of serious music and popular transcriptions. The reviews of this concert were moderately positive, with some serious reservations about programing and a lack of refined taste.

Oistrakh's next recital in the capital in 1933 was a real success. He performed concertos by Mozart, Mendelssohn and Tchaikovsky, and all Moscow critics pointed out his growing maturity and mastery.

In 1934, the deputy director of the Moscow Conservatory, Aleksander Goldenweiser, offered Oistrakh a position as an assistant professor, which the young violinist accepted. The following year, David won second prize at Heinrich Wieniawski Competition in Warsaw. Immediately after the competition, he made his first international tour, giving concerts in Poland, Hungary and Turkey, and his name became internationally known.

Oistrakh achieved even a bigger success at the 1937 Ysaÿe Competition in Brussels, where he won first prize. In the late 1930s, his performing style became individual and mature and he was fully equipped to extend his concert programs beyond the usual classical and romantic menu.

He started to collaborate with leading Soviet composers, encouraging them to compose for the violin. The result of these collaborations were very fruitful: in 1939, Oistrakh premièred the Violin Concerto by Nicolai Miaskovsky, Op. 44; and a year later he performed for the first time the Violin Concerto by Aram Khachaturian in D minor. Later, he gave premières of several compositions by Prokofiev and Shostakovich.

During World War II, Oistrakh played at the front, in hospitals, and in besieged Leningrad. At the end of the war, he met Yehudi Menuhin in Moscow, with whom David kept a close friendship and collaboration through the rest of his life. The duo of Oistrakh and Menuhin gave extensive concert tours throughout the world, but, surprisingly, never played together in the USSR.

In 1946 and 1947, Oistrakh gave a cycle of concerts in Moscow entitled "The Development of the Violin Concerto." Along with concertos by Bach, Mozart, Beethoven, Mendelssohn, Brahms, Dvorák, and Tchaikovsky he also performed concertos by Sibelius, Elgar and Walton which were almost unknown at that time in the USSR.

After World War II, Oistrakh renewed his international concert career. In 1951, he was in Brussels as a member of the jury of the Queen Elizabeth Competition, first prize of which went to the twenty-seven-year-old Leonid Kogan. After the competition Oistrakh performed concertos by Bach, Mozart and Beethoven and re-established his high international reputation.

In November of 1955, he made his American début in New York's Carnegie Hall. Among other musical dignitaries, the eighty-year-old Fritz Kreisler attended this concert. Oistrakh remembered:

> When I saw the great violinist, who listened to me with concentration, then gave me standing applause, I imagined this as a marvellous dream. After the concert Kreisler dropped into my dressing-room to congratulate me on my success.[5]

During that tour, Oistrakh gave the American première of the Violin Concerto No. 1, Op. 77 by Shostakovich, performing it on December 29th, 1955 with the New York Philharmonic under the baton of Dimitri Mitropoulos.

In the 1960s, Oistrakh returned to the USA six more times, giving many recitals and playing with the leading American orchestras and conductors. He also toured Western Europe annually, sometimes several times per year, and participated in many prestigious festivals. The violinist continued his tireless concert activity within the USSR as well. In his career, he gave concerts in more than 180 Soviet cities and towns, visiting some of them on several occasions.

During his long performing career, Oistrakh collaborated with several fine accompanists. Before World War II it was Vsevolod Topilin, a brilliant pianist and a chamber-music player. Topilin's career was abruptly broken during the war, when he was captured by the Germans and became a prisoner of war. Upon returning to Russia, he was accused of treason, sent to a labour camp and never returned to the concert stage. After the war Oistrakh performed with such pianists as Vladimir Yampolsky, Abram Makarov and Frieda Bauer.

The violinist had special love for chamber music. Among his partners were many great musicians, including Sviatoslav Richter, Paul Badura-Skoda, Lev Oborin, and his own son Igor Oistrakh. As early as in 1941, Oistrakh formed a trio consisting of himself, Lev Oborin (piano) and Sviatoslav Knushevitsky (cello). They gave extensive concerts throughout the USSR, though their tours abroad were quite rare. In the 1950s and 1960s, they were the best Soviet trio, enjoying tremendous popularity.

Oistrakh also often played as a member of a string quartet that included Pyotr Bondarenko (second violin), Michael Tarian (viola) and Sviatoslav Knushevitsky (cello). Many of their performances were broadcast by the USSR radio.

In 1967 began Oistrakh's collaboration with Sviatoslav Richter. In July of that year, the reviewer of their concert at the Lyon Festival wrote: "We found that the soloist enjoyed unlimited and dominated freedom, yet was ready to subdue it to the pianist. We were bewitched by the flexibility of the balance between them."[6]

Considering that they each had a saturated concert schedule, it was amazing how Oistrakh and Richter were able to find time to prepare their programs. Responding to an invitation to play with Richter at the 1971 Salzburg Festival, Oistrakh wrote to its organizers: "I would gladly play with Richter at the Festival... if I meet him before it!"[7]

Despite difficulties Oistrakh and Richter gave performances in Moscow, Leningrad, Lyon, Tours, London, Paris, Salzburg, New York, and Philadelphia. Their programs included sonatas by Beethoven, Brahms, Bartók and Shostakovich.

Oistrakh's repertoire was huge and consisted of hundreds of baroque, classical, romantic and contemporary compositions. His contemporary repertoire was much more diverse than those of many other

Soviet violinists and included such names as Stravinsky, Kodály, Bartók, Janácek, Hindemith, Ravel, Szymanowski, Sibelius, Elgar, Walton, Prokofiev, Shostakovich, Khachaturian, Miaskovsky, Dmitri Kabalevsky, Nicolai Rakov and Moisei Vaynberg.

Oistrakh gave the première of many compositions of Western composers in the USSR as well as world premières of many compositions by Soviet composers. His reputation as a popularizer of Soviet violin music was widely recognized, and Khachaturian and Miaskovsky dedicated concertos to him. He also received the dedication of both Violin Concertos by Shostakovich (No I, Op. 77 and No 2, Op. 129) as well as Sonatas by Prokofiev (No I, Op. 80) and Shostakovich (Op. 134).

At the peak of his performing career, in the 1950s and 1960s, Oistrakh particularly liked playing Beethoven, Brahms and Shostakovich, and their compositions appeared very often on his concert programs.

Oistrakh began to make recordings relatively late, only after World War II. However, considering that he recorded more than 350 compositions, his discography would place him among a few most recorded violinists. He recorded nearly all the major nineteenth and twentieth-century violin concertos, including those of Mendelssohn, Beethoven, Brahms, Dvoøák, Tchaikovsky, Glazunov, Bruch, Szymanowski, Bartók, Prokofiev, Khachaturian, Sibelius, Stravinsky, Shostakovich, and Hindemith. Oistrakh's list of sonata recordings is also immense. Among his outstanding achievements, the Sonatas by Tartini (*Devil's Trill*), Prokofiev (No I, Op. 80 and No 2, Op. 94), Shostakovich (Op. 134), and Khachaturian No 3 (in G minor) are of special note.

In 1962 in Paris, Oistrakh and Oborin performed publicly and recorded all ten of Beethoven's sonatas in a studio. Oistrakh remembered:

> We worked hard, did not go out, kept from tempting walks through the city, and rejected numerous invitations for parties. We wanted to stay with Beethoven's music, to think again on the sonatas' structure, to go through each detail. Our listeners did not get any more pleasure than we did. We enjoyed each evening when we played sonatas on the stage; we were happy to listen to this music in the silence of a studio, where the most favourable conditions were provided for us.[8]

Even today this recording has few rivals in its range of colour, nuance and mood.

Speaking of Oistrakh's performing style, one should think of him as a great story-teller. He could render the most complicated composition so logically and intelligently that it became understandable even to ordinary listeners. The violinist was an objective story-teller, delivering the composer's story rather than his own version of it.

His tone was always natural and effortless. No one could find any seams in his playing, even when he executed the most difficult passages. Oistrakh's son Igor remembered:

> My father possessed an extraordinary technique which gave him an opportunity to sight-read any composition. His hands were always "warmed up". Having got up in the morning, he first of all took his violin out of its case and played a few of the most difficult passages at a dizzying speed and with perfect clarity. His playing was so natural and unlaboured that he never had corns on the fingers of his left hand, which many violinists have.[9]

Oistrakh avoided romantic overexpressiveness; his emotions, although deep and penetrating, were always under control and displayed a refined taste. Clarity of statement, the inner logic of the composition, its structure and style were always his priorities, and in this regard he was a modern, post-romantic performer. To achieve complete clarity, he avoided very fast tempi, although his tremendous technique allowed him to compete on equal terms with all renowned virtuosi. This characteristic feature of Oistrakh's performances was highly praised by Fritz Kreisler, who once said: "My friend possesses the most important quality: he plays slow. This is unusual, because we live at the age of money, power, force and speed."[10]

Oistrakh's stage behaviour avoided any mannerism. He had confidence in the audience and did not miss any opportunity to show it. He would appear at the stage door with a big smile, and kept smiling while walking to the centre of the stage. It sent a clear signal that the artist loved his audience and would like to play for it. Then, as he was tuning his violin and during the ensuing performance, his face would become serious and absorbed. A big friendly smile would appear again when the performance was over and David was bowing.

Oistrakh always felt utmost responsibility towards the audience and was a very reliable performer. Unlike such artists as Richter, Horowitz, and Michelangeli, he did not rely on the creative mood only and was in good concert form at any time. Cancellations of his concerts were extremely rare and could be caused only by a serious illness. Of course, like any human being, he was from time to time under the influence of quite negative stresses; but even then, thanks to his iron self-discipline, tremendous mastery, and experience, he managed to maintain almost perfect performances.

As a violin teacher, Oistrakh can be compared with the great Leopold Auer. As an assistant professor and then a professor at the Moscow Conservatory for forty years, Oistrakh taught hundreds of graduates and post-graduates. During his last years at the Conservatory he was free of routine teaching duties such as technique development or studying compositions with his students. All these responsibilities were transferred to his assistants, among whom were such outstanding violinists as Piotr Bondarenko, Igor Oistrakh, Victor Pikaisen, Olga Kaverzneva and Simeon Snitkovsky. Oistrakh himself devoted his time and efforts to interpreting compositions and developing students' imagination and individuality. He often told his students with undeveloped creative initiative: "Do not accompany your accompanist."[11] Another piece of Oistrakh's advice was: " Do not be afraid to argue with the composer, and you will find what is your own."[12]

In order not to oppress the student's individual performing style or create performing clichés, Oistrakh in his last teaching years preferred verbal explanations of how to interpret a composition rather than showing directly how it should be played.

His teaching approach was very delicate; he always tried to convince rather than to order. It is not surprising that so many personalities with such diverse performing styles graduated from his class at the Moscow Conservatory. Among them were such names as Nina Beilina, Stefan Gheorgiu, Eduard Grach, Olga Kaverzneva, Oleg Kagan, Valery Klimov, Gidon Kremer, Oleg Krisa, Igor Oistrakh, Olga Parkhomenko, Victor Pikaisen, Simeon Snitkovsky, and Liana Isakadze. Many became either winners or finalists at many prestigious international violin competitions.

Overloaded with heavy concert schedules, teaching responsibilities and various administrative and public duties, Oistrakh usually worked to the edge of his physical ability. Among the few hobbies he could allow himself, chess was a favourite. The violinist was an advanced amateur chess player, and whenever he had time, he liked to challenge his colleagues at the chessboard. It is interesting to note that before World War II, Oistrakh played "a match" with another chess lover, Sergei Prokofiev. It took place at the Central Artists' House in Moscow and complied with the time limit established for official matches. Later Oistrakh remembered: "...the participants were as nervous as if they were playing for the world championship."[13]

Like some other great performers of the twentieth century, Oistrakh did not avoid "the conducting fever". His extensive knowledge of both the violin and symphonic literature, as well as some natural conducting instinct, contributed to his desire to be a conductor. He took the podium for the first time on February 17th, 1962, at the Great Hall of the Moscow Conservatory. At this concert, the Moscow Philharmonic with Igor Oistrakh as a soloist, performed Violin Concertos by Bach, Beethoven and Brahms under David's baton. This concert was a great success for both musicians and a good starting point for Oistrakh Senior's conducting career. Gradually, he extended into symphonic repertoire which included symphonies by Beethoven, Schubert, Brahms, Tchaikovsky, Mahler, Prokofiev, Shostakovich. In 1966 in Vienna, Oistrakh conducted all symphonies, concertos and *The German Requiem* by Brahms, one of his favourite composers.

David Oistrakh was decorated with many awards both in the USSR and abroad. He was a Stalin and Lenin prize winner. He also received the title of "People's Artist of the USSR", the highest title for a Soviet artist. He held honorary diplomas and awards from the Royal Academy of Music in London, the Academy Santa Cecilia in Rome, and the American Academy of Arts and Sciences. The violinist also received a doctorate in music *Honoris Causa* from Oxford University.

Oistrakh belonged to the Soviet musical establishment and it left an imprint on many of his speeches and publications. However, in some critical situations he and a certain degree of independence from the official position of the Soviet authorities. In 1948, he did not sign the letter condemning Shostakovich and Prokofiev for 'formalism' and the 'anti-national' character of their compositions. This letter was signed by many Soviet cultural dignitaries and published in the Communist Party's mouthpiece *Pravda*. On a personal level, Oistrakh expressed his support to the ostracized Shostakovich and gave him various sorts of encouragement. In 1967, during and after the Six Day War in the Middle East, the Soviet press undertook an unprecedented anti-Israeli campaign, in which many outstanding Russian musicians were involved. Significantly, Oistrakh never signed any letters or statements condemning "Israeli aggression." In many of his public speeches and numerous articles, Oistrakh expressed his respect for distinguished Western composers and performers, regardless of their political orientation. Under the totalitarian Soviet regime, even such a minor departure from the official cultural doctrine could be quite dangerous.

The great violinist suddenly passed away on October 24th, 1974, in Amsterdam from a severe heart attack.

A year after his untimely death, Sviatoslav Richter and Oleg Kagan gave a special concert in Moscow to commemorate the who man had been a colleague and teacher. They performed Beethoven's Sonatas Nos. 2, 4 and 5, which David had often played; but, symbolically, the opening piece on that memorable evening was the unfinished Sonata in A major by Mozart.

Yehudi Menuhin said on Oistrakh's death: "He was a musician and a human being who was able to deliver to other people his own deep thoughts and emotions, as well as those of composers and his people, who suffered so much."[14]

Notes

1.   Soroker, Y., *David Oistrakh (David Oistrakh)*, Jerusalem, 1981, p. 9.

2.   Ibid., p. 64.

3.   Markiz., L., *David Oistrakh (David Oistrakh)*, Moscow, 1977, p. 12.

4.   Soroker, Y., op. cit., p. 26.

5.   Ibid., p. 69.

6.   Uzefovich, V., *David Oistrakh: Besedy s Igorem Oistrakhom (David Oistrakh: Conversations with Igor Oistrakh)*, Sovetskiy Kompozitor, Moscow, 1978, p. 299.

7.   See note 6.

8.   Tsypin, G., *Portrety sovetskykh pianistov (Portraits of Soviet Pianists)*, Sovetskiy Kompozitor, Moscow, 1990, p.78.

9.   Soroker, Y., op. cit., p. 74.

10.   Ibid., p. 72.

11.   Ibid., p. 135.

12.   Ibid., p. 143.

13.   Markiz, L., op. cit., p. 16.

14.   Soroker, Y., op. cit., p. 167.

A SHINING TALENT

A SHORT, STOCKY MAN WITH CARE- fully brushed, abundant red hair and penetrating brown eyes, Gilels' stage appearance was impressive. As he stepped on stage, audiences sensed that he was a man with a strong will and intense energy. His position at the piano was absolutely natural; even when playing at the fastest tempos, he never fought with the instrument, rather seeming to give it a big, friendly hug.

Emil Gilels

Gilels performed with an astonishing technique and a glorious sonority. At forte level, the pianist was never percussive, but no orchestra could overpower him. His playing was flawless, with practically no wrong notes. Anton Rubinstein once said that he played enough incorrect notes in one recital to make up another one, but all Gilels' missed and wrong notes would barely make a piano miniature.

Emil Gilels' father, a low-paid clerk in an Odessa sugar factory, lost his first wife, then married a widow with two children. Born from this second marriage were two future musicians—Emil in 1916 and Elizabeth in 1919. The family suffered financially as a consequence of political turmoil in the city, which was captured several times by the opposing forces during the Civil War in 1918-1920. A wave of terror, deterioration of the economy, and severe food shortages accompanied each change of power. Due to their of financial pressures, Gilels' parents spent little time with their children. As a toddler, Emil's entertainment came from pressing an old piano's keys and listening to the magical combination of sounds.

By the age of five, Emil Gilels began studying with Jacob Tkach, the pupil of French virtuoso Raoul Pugno. After studying with Tkach for eight years, Gilels developed an advanced technique and extensive repertoire. He had several lessons each week, which began with various scales, and it was these excersises that helped to develop finger dexterity, fluency, and the ability to use various touches, ranging from crystalline to dramatic. The pianist retained this early love of scales for the rest of his life. Many years later, Gilels wrote: "Every morning I approach my toolbox and choose those tools without which I can never work. They are scales in direct and contrary motions, scales in thirds, sixths, and tenths."

Tkach's main concern was technical perfection rather than interpretation or excellence of style, and his lessons were unconventional. He insisted that students should sight-read each new piece by playing it with each hand separately. The next step was to play segments of the piece with both hands and then combine all these segments together. Only after completing these steps did students memorize the piece. With great care, Tkach indicated all the nuances, pedaling, and fingering in the score.

The result of studying with Tkach was twofold: Gilels received professional musical training and developed technique through persistent daily work at the instrument, but at the same time, his musical development was limited. He never played the music of Bach, Handel, Mozart, Haydn, or any Russian composers, and at the age of 13, Gilels was as yet unfamiliar with symphonic and operatic literature.

Despite these deficiencies, the music world should credit Tkach for noting Gilels' talent. In 1925 he wrote:

> I would like to confirm that my nine-year old pupil, Gilels, is a child prodigy. He possesses remarkable hands and outstanding hearing, characteristic features of those who were born to play piano. If he is provided with reasonably good living conditions, the boy

will be able to get the musical training required for the further development of his talent. If society helps him in this regard, we shall witness the rise of an outstanding virtuoso who will please audiences. In the future, the USSR will have a pianist of world-class calibre.[1]

For his début at age 13, Gilels performed Beethoven's "Pathetique" Sonata as well as compositions of Scarlatti, Schumann, Chopin, and Mendelssohn. Twenty years later, the renowned Ukrainian composer Konstantin Dankevich recalled this recital: "Even at that time, we felt the tremendous grasp, iron rhythm, mighty energy, and sunny temperament of the 13-year old pianist."[2]

In 1927, Gilels entered the Odessa Conservatory and worked with Bertha Reingbald,[3] the teacher of such well-known Russian pianists as Tatyana Goldfarb, Ludmila Sosina, Bertha Maranz, Heinrietta Mirvis, Oscar Feltsman and Samuel Choklin. She had a profound influence on young Gilels, who viewed her as a second mother and adored her for the rest of his life. Indeed, Gilels spent more time in her apartment than at home. A perfect tutor as well as a loving and caring person, Reingbald widened Gilels' musical horizon to include more lyrical pieces, not just virtuoso and bravura music as Tkach did.

The pianist began to study Bach's music and other masters of polyphony and to explore the classical operatic and symphonic repertoire vigorously. Recalling those years, Gilels wrote in 1964:

> Reingbald was both a great piano teacher and a great educator, and this combination was highly beneficial for her students. Not only did she teach them music, but she also heartily loved all of them. A sensitive psychologist, she could unmistakably define students' potentials and rouse their desire for development to the highest level.[4]

Gilels' years in the conservatory were not easy. The young musician was required to perform frequently to ease the family's financial hardship, playing a lot of light music in order to satisfy the tastes of audiences, which distracted him from regular studies with Reingbald. The situation improved in 1931, when Gilels won the Ukrainian Competition and earned a special scholarship from the government.

In the spring of 1933, Gilels, accompanied by Reingbald, went to Moscow to participate in the All-Union Competition, where the unknown 16-year-old pianist won first prize and achieved instant notoriety. His career skyrocketed, and he signed numerous contracts with Soviet concert agencies. As a result, the pianist assumed a breakneck schedule of concerts spending most of his time touring the Soviet Union. Gilels performed so often during these two years that he had no time to enrich his repertoire and sometimes performed compositions that were not fully prepared. Even a phenomenal technique proved to be of little help and flaws became apparent to audiences. During a 1935 Moscow tour Gilels' performance of the Tchaikovsky Piano Concerto No I received several harsh reviews in the capital's newspapers. It was a clear, alarming signal for the young pianist, who consequently decided to quit the concert stage. He returned to Odessa and graduated from the Conservatory in November of 1935.

At year's end, Gilels departed for the Moscow Conservatory to work with Heinrich Neuhaus, who helped him to polish his skills and musical style for another three years. In 1936, Gilels took second prize at the Vienna Competition and two years later became the first-prize winner at the prestigious Ysaÿe Competition in Brussels. Gilels started to teach at the Moscow Conservatory in 1938 and became a full professor in 1952.

During World War II, the pianist played extensively for servicemen at military bases, on warships, and in hospitals. He flew to Leningrad in the late fall of 1943 to perform in the unheated Philharmonic Hall for the city's exhausted inhabitants.

In the 1940s and 1950s Gilels' enthusiasm for chamber music led to a collaboration with his sister, Elizabeth, on the Sonatas of Vivaldi, Mozart, Haydn, and Cui for violin and piano, recordings still praised in Russia today. For 14 years, from 1939 to 1953, Gilels worked with another outstanding Soviet pianist, Yakov Zak,[5] as one of the best piano duos of the twentieth century. The mighty power of Gilels blended well with the refined lyricism of Zak.

After the war, Gilels performed throughout the USSR as well as in Eastern Europe and Western countries. He debuted in America in October 1955, performing Tchaikovsky's Piano Concerto No. I with Eugene Ormandy and the Philadelphia Orchestra. Gilels was the first Soviet artist to perform in North America in thirty-four years.

During the 1950s and 1960s, Gilels was a member of many juries at international competitions. In 1958, he was chair of the jury for the first Tchaikovsky Piano Competition in Moscow, which awarded Van Cliburn the gold medal. Six years later, the jury of the third Tchaikovsky Piano Competition, again chaired by Gilels, awarded first prize to the barely known sixteen-year-old Grigory Sokolov from Leningrad.

Gilels continued to tour and teach at the Moscow Conservatory. As a teacher, he never imposed his creative ideas on students but helped them define, develop and nourish their own musical personalities. He never insisted that a student's interpretation be the same as his own. Among his students were Vladimir Block, Igor Zhukov, the second-prize winner at the 1956 Marguerite Long Competition in Paris, and Marina Mdivani, the first-prize winner at the same Competition in 1961.

Gilels' first wife was pianist Rose Tamarkina, who died of cancer at the age of 30. His second marriage to Farizeth, bore a daughter, Elen in 1948. By 1972 Emil and Elen, who was also a pianist, often appeared on the concert stage together, performing Mozart's Concerto for two pianos and Schubert's piano duos. Elen Gilels died in 1996.

Emil Gilels joined the Communist Party at an early age but maintained some artistic independence from party authorities. He was the first Soviet artist to praise Nicolai Medtner's music, which was prohibited in the USSR, and even performed the composer's G minor Sonata. The pianist also revived *Petroushka* by Igor Stravinsky, another émigré composer whose compositions were banned from the concert stage by Soviet bureaucrats. Despite the government's promotion of anti-semitism, Gilels was among the first to popularize the music of Jewish composer Moisei Vaynberg[6]; he gave the première of his Piano Sonatas Nos. 2 and 4 and the Piano Quintet.

Gilels received all the highest awards in the USSR, including the Stalin and Lenin prizes, the gold medal of the Hero of Socialist Labour, and the title of "People's Artist of the USSR." He was also a member of the Royal Academy of Music in London, the Franz Liszt Academy in Budapest, and the Santa Cecilia Academy in Rome. Gilels died in Moscow on 14 October, 1985.

Throughout his musical career, Gilels was particularly attracted to large forms such as concertos and sonatas, and was apparently the only pianist to record all the Concertos of Beethoven, Brahms, and Tchaikovsky. Apart from these masterpieces, Gilels' repertoire was enormously abundant and included more than 400 compositions. He was particularly captivated when playing Beethoven's five Piano Concertos with such outstanding conductors as Otto Klemperer, Eugene Ormandy, André Cluytens, George Enescu, Kurt Sanderling, Yevgeny Mravinsky, George Szell, and Kurt Mazur. In February 1956, Gilels performed all five Concertos in a series of two evenings; this was the first time anyone had done this since 1927, when Arthur Schnabel took on the same ambitious project to commemorate the 100th anniversary of Beethoven's death. Following the Leningrad première, Gilels performed the five Concerto cycle throughout Russia, the United States, France, Bulgaria, and other countries. In December 1976, a critic in Leningrad wrote in *Sovetskaya muzika (The Soviet Music Magazine)*:

> Contemporaries of Beethoven testified that his playing was marked with power, brilliance, and liveliness. Contrary to this, Hummel demonstrated the highest purity, accuracy, grace, and tenderness. We can say with certainty that Gilels' performance combined all of these and much more.[7]

Gilels hoped to play all thirty-two Beethoven Piano Sonatas in a series of concerts, but unfortunately this project never came to fruition. However, he played many of the Sonatas often, including Nos. 8, 14 and 23, and interpreted these three masterpieces differently at each stage of his career. The young Gilels used extremely fast tempos and ferocious sounds, while as a mature pianist he demonstrated genuine, balanced and convincing expressivity, free of emotional exaggerations.

In the 1970s and 1980s, the pianist played many of Schumann's pieces, including the Toccata, *Carnaval, Kreisleriana,* and Symphonic Etudes, rendering these compositions with technical perfection, poetry, and passion. In 1975, at a Festival in Bergen, he performed the 20 Lyric Pieces of Edward Grieg, revealing a new emotional side of his playing. He referred to them saying, "They are not simple children's pictures. This music is very intimate. The sincerity and lyricism of each miniature has captivated me. The selection of these pieces and their programming have brought me a real joy." Indeed, Gilels' performance of Grieg is deeply sincere, coloured with a melancholic sadness and filled with carefully chiseled details that have gone unnoticed by many other performers.

Among Russian composers, Gilels played more Tchaikovsky and Rachmaninoff than most. He was one of the best performers of the Tchaikovsky Piano Concerto No I, recording it with such conductors as Samuel Samosud, Sixten Ehrling, Fritz Reiner, Karel Ancerl, Fernando Previtali, Pedro Freitas Branco de, Yevgeny Svetlanov, Yevgeny Mravinsky, Zubin Mehta, Colin Davis, and Lorin Maasel. The indomitable power in its first and third movements and the improvisatory freedom in the slow, second movement captivated listeners. The pianist also frequently performed the lesser known Second and Third Concertos by Tchaikovsky.

Gilels' performance of the Rachmaninoff Concerto No 3 with the Paris Conservatory Symphony under the direction of André Cluytens is noble and more musically restrained than that of Vladimir Horowitz; it demonstrates dazzling emotional and technical control. American pianist, critic and broadcaster David Dubal notes that upon Gilels' visit to The Juilliard School in 1955, a student asked how long it took him to learn the Rachmaninoff Third: "I began work on it at the age of 18, and I am still working on it,"[8] replied the pianist.

Although nineteenth-century music was the core of Gilels' repertoire, he was comfortable playing the French Impressionists and contemporary music as well. During later years he performed a lot of Debussy and Ravel with extreme purity, elegance, and a refined sense of colour. Gilels' Prokofiev was also technically superb and convincing. He performed *Visions Fugitives*, the Third Concerto, the Toccata, and the Second, Third, Seventh, and Eighth Sonatas. The last was dedicated to Gilels, who premiered it in Moscow on the 30th of December, 1945.

Gilels' piano ability was monumental and his performances charged listeners with optimism, energy, and vivacity. Gilels' shining talent is remembered by those who heard his live performances, and his numerous recordings testify to his grand manner, and startling technique.

Notes

1. Khentova, S., *Emil Gilels* (Khentova, S.,*Emil Gilels*), Sovetskiy Kompozitor, Moscow, 1959, p. 13.

2. See note 1.

3. Reingbald, Bertha (1897-1944), a piano teacher. She graduated from the Odessa Conservatory in 1919 and started to teach at this Conservatory in 1921. Reingbald became professor in 1933 and Dean of the Piano Faculty in 1938. Together with P. Stolyarsky she was a co-founder of the Odessa music school for gifted children in 1933. In 1939-1941 she served as Head of Performing Section of the USSR Composers' Union.

4. *Gordost' sovetskoy muziki* (*The Pride of Soviet Music*), Edited by Michail Yakovlev, Sovetskiy Kompozitor, Moscow, 1987, p. 81.

5. Zak, Yakov (1913-1976), a pianist and teacher. He studied piano with Maria Starkova at the Odessa Conservatory (1930-1932) and then with Heinrich Neuhaus at the Moscow Conservatory (1933-1935). He won the third prize at the All-Union Competition in Moscow in 1935 and the first prize at the Chopin Competition in Warsaw in 1937. Zak concertized intensively around the world and taught piano. He became professor at the Moscow Conservatory in 1947 and Dean of its Piano Faculty in 1965. Among his students were Heinrietta Mirvis, Yevgeny Mogilevsky, Nicolai Petrov, Yuri Egorov and Alexander Toradze. Zak was awarded the title of "People's Artist of the USSR" in 1966. He premiered works of many Soviet composers, including Yevgeny Golubev, Yury Levitin, Dmitri Kabalevsky, Marian Koval' and Michail Chulaki.

6. Vaynberg, Moisei (1919-1996), a composer. He graduated from the Warsaw Conservatory; in 1939 he moved to the USSR and graduated from the Minsk Conservatory. As "a Jewish nationalist", Vaynberg was imprisoned in 1953 and released after Stalin's death. Among his compositions were several op-

eras, oratorios, 20 symphonies, several concertos for various instruments, 22 sonatas, chamber, vocal and incidental music. Many of his compositions are based on Jewish folk and religious tunes. In 1980, he was awarded the title of "People's Artist of the Russian Federation."

7.   *Sovetskaya muzika* (*The Soviet Music Magazine*), December, 1976.

8   Dubal, D., *The Art of the Piano*, A Harvest Book, Harcourt Brace & Company, San Diego, New York, London, 1995, p.92.

11

SVIATOSLAV RICHTER

A PIANIST FOR ALL SEASONS

THE FAMOUS PRE-WAR SOVIET piano school produced such outstanding pianists as Yakov Zak, Isaac Mikhnovsky, Yakov Flier, Anatoly Vedernikov, Victor Merzhanov, Tatyana Nikolaeva, Vladimir Sofronitsky, Lev Oborin, and Maria Yudina. Above this group of world-class performers, Sviatoslav Richter still towers above almost all, for his profound interpretations and breathtaking technique.

Born in Ukraine on March 20th, 1915, Sviatoslav was the son of a pianist, organist, and composer, Theophile Richter, who had studied in Vienna and later taught piano at the Odessa Conservatory. Sviatoslav learned a rudimentary theory and piano performance from his father, but had little formal training. He was largely self-taught and improvised intensively, sight-reading piano and opera music. Sviatoslav also studied composition, composed songs, and read the classical Russian and West European literature. He even wrote plays and started to paint.

Sviatoslav Richter

In 1931, Richter became the accompanist for the Odessa Philharmonic Society and, two years later, for the Odessa Opera and Ballet Theatre. Although young Richter was pleased with this appointment, his dream was to become an opera conductor, not a pianist. He diligently studied the classical and modern opera repertoire and worked with vocalists and the chorus. Richter made his piano début in May 1934 with an all-Chopin program in Odessa. Despite his lack of any concert experience, reviewers were impressed with his outstanding talent and striking technique.

Richter's conducting career never materialized in Odessa, and he eventually focused completely on piano playing. In 1937, he moved to Moscow to study with Heinrich Neuhaus. On many occasions Richter acknowledged his debt to this great teacher. After Neuhaus' death in 1964 Richter writing: "I became his student by chance. However, I got not only a teacher but a second father. When I talk about him, I am afraid to destroy by words the charm and aura of his elusive and beautiful image."[1] Neuhaus expressed admiration for Richter throughout his life and wrote to a student in 1959, "Slava Richter gave a concert today, and his performance was unbelievably beautiful. It contained a real spirituality and passion. Our young people often think that passion starts below the navel. How they are misled!"[2] Shortly before his death, Neuhaus wrote to a relative in Germany, "Richter gave a fabulous concert of Handel, Hindemith, and Shostakovich. The recital hall was packed as usual and unable to accommodate all the listeners who wanted to hear Slava. He is a genius."[3]

Richter gave his first recital in Moscow in 1942 and performed extensively in the capital in the 1940s and 1950s. His playing was vivid and inspired, though some of his interpretations were strained and his fortes often sounded forced.

The musician graduated from the Moscow Conservatory in 1944 with a gold medal and shared first prize at the 1945 Third All-Union Competition in Moscow with Victor Merzhanov. In the second round of that competition, Richter played Liszt's *Wilde Jagd ("Wild Chase")* when the electricity was suddenly cut off. Stagehands placed candles on the grand piano, and Richter continued playing. When he performed the tremendous crescendo and fortissimo at the finale, his energetic hand movements blew all the candles out, so he finished the performance in complete darkness.

Despite his victory at this prestigious competition, Richter's life in Moscow was difficult and unsettled until the mid-1950s. He had neither his own apartment nor a piano at his disposal, and Soviet authorities did not allow him to go on concert tours abroad until after Stalin's death in 1953.

In 1946, Richter married a fine soprano, Nina Dorliak, with whom he collaborated for many years in concert and on recordings. Among the many concerts he gave in the 1940s and early 1950s, two performances are noteworthy. On the 9th of May, 1946, he dedicated a concert to the 55th birthday of Sergei Prokofiev, performing the composer's Sonatas Nos. 6, 7, and 8. Moscow critics unanimously acknowledged him as one of the best of Prokofiev's interpreters. On April 21st, 1951, Richter gave the première performance of Prokofiev's Sonata No 9, which was dedicated to the pianist, to commemorate the composer's 60th birthday.

Sviatoslav Richter made his conducting début on February 18th, 1952, with the Moscow Youth Symphony performing Prokofiev's Concertino for cello and orchestra. The cello soloist was a young Mstislav Rostropovich. This was Richter's first and last appearance as a conductor. Heinrich Neuhaus wrote about Richter as a conductor: "The great conductor has not realized himself. He possesses a special feeling of the musical form and its rhythmical structure. He introduces a harmony that originates from the classical perception of the music. Everybody should dream of him going back to the stage and conducting again."

Richter had exceptional natural gifts. His sight-reading ability was extraordinary - even when sight-reading the most difficult score, it was delivered as a refined concert performance. His memory was supernatural - at the peak of his career he was able to perform any of more than eighty concert programs at a few days' notice. The pianist also knew by heart a huge part of the operatic and symphonic repertoire, including operas by Wagner, Strauss, and Mozart, symphonies by Mahler, Bruckner, and Beethoven as well as tone poems by Strauss, Debussy and Scriabin.

But this was not all. Richter was a very gifted painter, and his remarkable talent was recognized and praised by such an authority as the outstanding Russian artist Robert Fal'k. The pianist's earlier experiments in the field of composition were also promising. However, he devoted his life to piano-playing and concentrated all his creative abilities in this specific field.

In the late 1950s, Richter gave numerous concerts in the USSR, but despite this busy schedule, continued polishing and extending his enormous repertoire. The pianist started touring abroad in 1953, first in Eastern European countries and China and then in Western Europe. In the fall of 1960, he gave his first North American concert in Chicago, performing the Brahms Concerto No 2 with the Chicago Symphony under the baton of Erich Leinsdorf. In late October, he gave five recitals in Carnegie Hall. The music critic David Dubal wrote: "I was at each event and was staggered by the glory of his garden. From Haydn and Beethoven, to Debussy and Ravel, Chopin and Schumann, Scriabin, Liszt, Szymanowski, Prokofiev, and more, he played it all with an intensity and purpose never to be forgotten. Richter seemed to be an apparition."[4]Richter toured the United States for ten weeks and gave 30 concerts.

In the 1960s Richter also toured Canada, Japan, Turkey, and Latin America. At that time, his quirkiness had become legendary: he hated the telephone; never remembered his home number; and he feared airplanes and trains. During a concert tour, Richter would disappear for days, worrying his agents until returning in time for his next performance. Like Horowitz, Richter believed that a routine performance was the worst thing for a musician; he preferred not to appear on the concert stage when he was not in a creative mood. As a result, he cancelled concerts and kept an unpredictable concert schedule: he could give several recitals in a city, then not return for many years. Richter liked to play in small Russian and European towns rather than in big cities. After some concerts, he did not play encores at all, but in a creative mood he might play numerous encores.

His practising schedule was also unusual. Sometimes the pianist did not touch the piano for weeks, but then some musical idea might inspire him to practise through the night after a concert. From 1981, Richter had followed the tradition of the nineteenth century and played with music on the concert stage. He also requested that the light should be directed toward the piano and turned off in the concert hall during his performance.

Unlike many other concert pianists, Richter liked playing chamber music, and collaborated with such famous musicians as David Oistrakh, Mstislav Rostropovich, Oleg Kagan, Dietrich Fischer-Dieskau, and the Borodin and Bolshoi Theatre String Quartets.

One of his most beloved "babies" was the Music Festival in the Grange de Meslay near Tours in France, of which Richter was a founder. Starting in 1964, for a few weeks in the summer season, a thirteenth-century barn in the middle of a cornfield was converted into a concert hall. The pianist played here each year until his death. Besides himself, artists of the calibre of Pierre Boulez, Daniel Barenboim, Lorin Maazel, Yury Bashmet, Natalia Gutman, and Dietrich Fischer-Dieskau figured among the participants in the festival which became increasingly popular among music-lovers in Europe and elsewhere.

Late in 1986, Richter went on a historic concert tour that he considered to be a special mission. For six months, he drove across the USSR twice, first eastwards from Novgorod to Khabarovsk, and then in the opposite direction from Khabarovsk to Saratov on the Volga River. During this unique 20,000-km marathon tour he gave 150 concerts for people who had never attended a live piano concert before Richter's appearance. His programs were not meant to entertain audiences but rather to enlighten and educate them. They included five Sonatas by Haydn, 33 Variations on a Waltz by Diabelli and Sonata No. 28 by Beethoven, Variations on the Theme by Paganini, Sonatas No 1 and No 2 by Brahms, *Nachtstücke*, *Blumenstück*, Twelve Concert Etudes after Caprices of Paganini and Toccata by Schumann, and all the Ballades and fifteen Etudes by Chopin.

Despite his age, Richter continued to explore new ways of delivering his art to audiences. In the late 1980s, he established a series of evening concerts in the Pushkin Museum in Moscow. Music-lovers called them "Richter Evenings" because the famous musician appeared on the stage every evening during this festival either as a soloist or with a chamber ensemble. It became a tradition to premiere new compositions of contemporary Russian and Western composers and to bring new performers to the concert stage of the Pushkin Museum.

In 1992, Richter established the Tarussa Richter Fund to support young artists. Tarussa is a small Russian town northeast of Moscow where the pianist spent his summers. The fund subsidizes master classes, performances and art exhibitions and supports the local music school in Tarussa. In 1993, the fund organized a music festival dedicated to the 150th birthday of Edvard Grieg for which Richter played as a soloist and an accompanist with a fine young soprano, Galina Pisarenko, the former pupil of Nina Dorliak.

In March of 1995, Richter turned eighty. However, his concert obligations remained so intense that many much younger pianists would have been unable to fulfil these. At the beginning of April of the previous year, Richter finished a two-month tour through Japan that included a special recital at the Yamaha headquarters in the city of Hamamatsu. In the middle of April, Richter performed in Seoul, where he gave a recital and played Concerto No 6 by Mozart with the Korean National Symphony. By the end of April the pianist was in Europe for a series of concerts in Germany, and in May he toured Switzerland. The following month, Richter was in the Grange de Meslay, the place he loved so much, playing with the Borodin Quartet. In July he opened a Festival in Germany commemorating the late violinist Oleg Kagan, with whom Sviatoslav had collaborated for fifteen years. The pianist spent his summer break near Hamburg, practising daily for several hours. In October, Richter gave several concerts in Munich, then drove to Milan, where he played Concerto No 1 by Beethoven with the Berlin Philharmonic under the baton of Vladimir Ashkenazy. From Milan he drove to the tiny Italian town Azolo, the birthplace of the great actress Eleonore Duse, whose dramatic talent he greatly admired.

In the first two months of 1995, Richter gave 35 performances in Italy, Spain and Portugal. Altogether, from April, 1994 till March, 1995, the musician appeared on the concert stage more than 80 times. This meant being on the road for many hours, living in various hotels (he had never had his own accommodation in Europe). Even at the age of eighty, he loved this nomadic life of the concertizing artist and would not change it for anything else.

Richter passed away in Moscow after a massive heart attack on August 1st, 1997. His last words were: "I am too tired."

To commemorate the great musician, the Russian government established three Richter Grants for the students of the Moscow Conservatory who demonstrate outstanding achievements in studying piano.

A memorial museum was opened in the pianist's Moscow apartment, which exibits many of Richter's memorabilia, including his paintings.

Richter's repertoire was enormous. In 1948 he said:

> I do not have favourite compositions or composers, and I want to play plenty of compositions. It does not mean that I am very ambitious or unable to concentrate my efforts on any specific pieces. In fact, I love so many compositions and want to play all of them for my audience.[5]

Richter had played J.S. Bach through all phases of his long musical career. He performed only Bach originals, avoiding transcriptions by Liszt, Busoni, Godowsky, and Rachmaninoff, which he considered distortions of Bach's style. In programs, Richter often included the suites of Handel as well as the sonatas and concertos of Mozart, Haydn, and Beethoven; he liked to play such Romantic composers as Schubert, Weber, Schumann, Chopin, Liszt, and Brahms. Richter was a leading interpreter of the French Impressionists Debussy and Ravel; and among other twentieth-century Western composers, he played Bartók, Hindemith, Reger, Richard Strauss, and Gershwin. He was not an admirer of atonal music and played only a few pieces by Alban Berg. The pianist played the Russian piano repertoire extensively, performing works by Glinka, Mussorgsky, Tchaikovsky, Rimsky-Korsakov, Glazunov, Scriabin, Stravinsky, Rachmaninoff, Prokofiev, Miaskovsky, and Shostakovich.

Richter started to make recordings in 1948 and produced them more than any other pianist. While Horowitz and Gould preferred to record in a studio, Richter liked to record live during his performances. In the 1970s, Richter's recordings of well-known Schubert sonatas were a revelation with their unpretentious lyricism taking on the character of deep philosophical meditation. His rhythmic precision and incredible ability to unify what some called incoherent music, gave these sonatas structural unity.

In February, 1958, Richter recorded Mussorgsky's *Pictures at an Exhibition,* a work that showed a mature pianist at his best, with poetry, humour, and heroic power. Despite technical imperfections, the recording won several international awards and was a best-seller for years.

Sviatoslav Richter championed Tschaikovsky's piano music, recording the Piano Concerto No I, *The Seasons*, numerous miniatures, and the rarely performed Sonata in G major. His recordings of Rachmaninoff include the Piano Concertos Nos I and 2, Preludes, and *Etudes-Tableaux*, which he enriched with passion, energy, and vigour. In his unconventional interpretation of the Rachmaninoff Piano Concerto No 2, he played both the first and second movements much slower than traditionally, including performances by the composer himself. The spectrum of his emotions was brighter than that of Rachmaninoff, and a sense of serene pathos prevailed over tragedy.

Richter was one of the best interpreters of Prokofiev, recording Sonatas Nos. 2, 4, 6, 7, 8 and 9, Piano Concertos Nos. I and 5, and many other composer's pieces. The tremendous energy, virtuosity, long melodic lines, and lyricism that a pianist should have to perform Prokofiev's music were compatible with Richter's artistic temperament.

Music critics characterized Richter's performing style as a perfect balance between glaring emotions and refined intellectualism. In his early years, he sometimes played with a wild expressiveness, but his later concerts were more balanced, his interpretations highly philosophical in nature.

Always unconventional, Richter's interpretations stemmed from his commitment to the score and not from musical eccentricity. He avoided the well-established clichés and tried to discover new musical facets, even among the warhorses of the repertoire, for phrasing, pedaling, and counterpoint. Richter has said: "I do not like the musical analysis that kills your fantasy, and as such is an enemy of the art. Let us stop talking about music; let music express itself."

Richter was completely absorbed in a piece of music and possessed the rare ability to maintain the emotional tension throughout lengthy slow movements and bravura passages. He was not afraid of silence: rests were no less meaningful than notes and chords. Richter's piano technique can be compared to that of Rachmaninoff, Horowitz, and Gilels; when listening to him, nobody even thought about the technical difficulties he had to overcome. In Richter, the audience heard a musician committed to delivering the composer's conception in a clear way; he was not a fireworks virtuoso. Such a commitment was and remains a rarity on the concert stage. The famous Canadian pianist Glenn Gould wrote about Richter:

> I have always believed that it is possible to divide musical performers into two categories - those who seek to exploit the instruments they use, and those who do not. In the first category...one could find a place for such legendary characters as Liszt and Paganini, as well as any number of allegedly demonic virtuosi of more recent vintage. That category belongs to musicians who are determined to make us aware of their relationship to their instrument, whatever it happens to be; they allow that relationship to become the focus of attention. The second category...includes musicians who try to bypass the whole question of the performing mechanism, to create the illusion...of a direct link between themselves and a particular musical score and who, therefore, help the listeners to achieve a sense of involvement, not with the performance per se, but rather with the music itself. And I think that, in our time, there is no better example of that second kind of musician than Sviatoslav Richter.[6]

Notes

1.   *Genrikh Neygauz. Vospominaniya, pis'ma, materialy (Heinrich Neuhaus. Memoirs, Letters, Materials*, Compiled by E.P. Richter), IMIDZH, Moscow, 1992, p. 182.

2.   Ibid., p. 259.

3.   Ibid., p. 291.

4.   Dubal, D., *The Art of the Piano*, A Harvest Book, Harcourt Brace & Company, San Diego, New York, London, 1995, p. 210.

5.   Del'son, V., *Sviatoslav Richter (Sviatoslav Richter)*, Sovetskiy Kompozitor, Moscow, 1960, p. 14.

6.   Glenn Gould. "Sviatoslav Richter", *Glenn Gould,* vol. I (Fall 1995), p. 12.

BIBLIOGRAPHY

1.   Auer, Leopold, *My Life in Music*, New York, 1923.

2.   Bachmann, Otto, *Roza Kaufmann: Eine biographische Skizze, nebst einiger Rezensionen.* Odessa, 1885.

3.   Barenboim, Daniel, *A Life in Music.* London, 1991.

4.   Brodsky, Anna. *A Recollection of a Russian Home.* London, 1914.

5.   Cui, César. *Istoricheskaya literatura fortepiannoy muziki, lekcii Rubinsteina, 1888-1889.* St. Petersburg, 1889.

6.   Del'son, Victor. *Sviatoslav Richter.* Moscow, 1960.

7.   Dubal, David. *The Art of the Piano.* San Diego, New York, London, 1995.

8.   Glikman, Isaak (compilor). *Pis'ma k drugu: Dmitri Shostakovich —Isaaku Glikmanu.* Moscow-St. Petersburg, 1993.

9.   Gould, Glenn. "Sviatoslav Richter". *Glenn Gould, vol I* (Fall 1995).

10.Grigoriev, Lev and Platek, Yacov (compilors). *Sovremennye dirizhery.* Moscow, 1969.

11.Karatygin, Vyacheslav. "Semper idem." *Zhis'n iskusstva 51* (1923).

12. Katz, Boris (compilor). *"Raskat improvizatsiy"…Muzika v tvorchestve, sud'be i v dome Pasternaka.* Leningrad, 1991.

13.   Kerner, Estelle. "Nathan Milstein Brahmin with Violin." *High Fidelity Magazine*, November 1977.

14.   Khentova, Sofia. *Emil Gilels*. Moscow, 1959.

15.   Kirkpatrick, Ralph. "European Journal." *High Fidelity/Musical America 35* (November 1985).

16.   Knowles, Clifford. "Brodsky in Manchester." *Music Matter 21* (1986).

17.   Kuznetsov, Anatoly (compilor). *Maria Veniaminovna Yudina. Stat'i, vospominaniya, materialy*. Moscow, 1978.

18.   Kuznetsov, Anatoly. "Maria Yudina. Iz vospominaniy." *Novy mir 6* (1997).

19.   Landowska, Wanda et Lew, Henry. *La Musique Ancienne*. Paris, 1909.

20   Levitsky, Serge. "Rose Koffman-Pasternak: la mére du poéte." *Etudes Slaves et Est Europèenes 8* (1963).

21.   Maikapar, Aleksander. "Slovo o Vande Landowskoy." In *Vanda Landowskaya o muzike*. Moscow, 1991.

22.   Markiz, Lev. *David Oistrach*. Moscow, 1977.

23.   Melnik, Semion. *Anton i Nicolai Rubinsteiny*. Jerusalem, 1990.

24.   Milstein, Nathan and Volkov, Solomon. *From Russia to the West*. New York, 1990.

25.   Nest'ev, Israel and Edel'man Grigori (compilors). *Sergei Prokofiev 1953-1963. Stat'i imaterialy*. Moscow, 1962.

26. Neygauz, Genrikh. *Ob isskusstve fortepiannoy igry.* Moscow, 1958.

27. Osborn, Max. *Leonid Pasternak.* Warsaw, 1932.

28. Palmer, Larry. "The Concertos of Falla and Poulenc." *The Diapason 70* (1979).

29. Pasternak, Boris. *Selected Poems.* London, 1983.

30. Pasternak, Leonid. *Zapisi raznykh let.* Moscow, 1975.

31. Pasternak, Leonid. *The Memoirs of Leonid Pasternak.* London, Melbourne, New York, 1982.

32. Poulenc, Francis. *Entretiens avec Claude Rostand.* Paris, 1954.

33. Restout, Dènise (editor). *Landowska on Music.* New York, 1965.

34. Richter, Elena (compilor). *Genrikh Neygauz. Vospominaniya, pis'ma, materialy.* Moscow, 1992.

35. Rogel, Irma. "Memories of Landowska." *Clavier 19* (1980).

36 Rubinstein, Anton. *Literaturnoe nasledie.* Moscow, 1986.

37. Rubinstein, Anton. "Vospominaniya 1829-1889." *Russkay-astarina,* November 1889.

38. Sacks, Harvey. *Virtuoso.* London, 1982.

39. Schwarz, Boris. *Great Masters of the Violin.* New York, 1983.

40. Soria, Dorle. "Artistic Life." *High Fidelity/Musical America,* July 1974.

41. Soroker, Yakov. *David Oistrach.* Jerusalem, 1981.

42.	Tchaikovsky, Modest. *Zhizn' Petra Il'icha Tchaikovskogo.* Moscow, 1997.

43.	Thomason, Geoffrey. "The Brodsky Archive at the RNCN." *Brio 22* (1985).

44.	Tsypin, Gennadi. *Portrety sovetskykh pianistov.* Moscow, 1990.

45.	Uzefovich, Victor. *David Oistrach. Besedy s Igorem Oistrakhom.* Moscow, 1978.

46.	Volkov, Solomon. *Testimony: The Memoirs of Dmitri Shostakovich.* New York, 1979.

47.	Yakovlev, Michail (editor). *Gordost' sovetskoy muziki.* Moscow, 1987.

48.	Yudina, Maria. "Modest Petrovich Musorgskiy: Kartinki s vystavki." *Sovetskaya muzika 9* (1974).

49.	Zimjanina, Natalia (compilor). *Stanislav Neygauz. Vospominaniya, pis'ma, materialy.* Moscow, 1988.

MEMBER OF SCABRINI MEDIA

Quebec, Canada
2002